The Man

With the

$100,000

Breasts

The Man With the $100,000 Breasts

and Other Gambling Stories

Michael Konik

Huntington Press
Las Vegas, Nevada

The Man With the $100,000 Breasts
and Other Gambling Stories

Published by:
   Huntington Press
   3687 South Procyon Avenue
   Las Vegas, Nevada 89103
   ph: (702) 252-0655
   fax: (702) 252-0675

ISBN 0-929712-72-2

Cover Design: Jason Cox
Cover Images: Jason Cox, West Stock, and Digital Stock
Interior Production & Design: Bethany Coffey

"The Man With the $100,000 Breasts" originally appeared in *Maxim*; "1-900-NFL-SCAM" and "Shakin' Down the Sheiks" in *Forbes FYI*; "Go, Greyhound!" and "The Adventures of Huckleberry Seed" in *Un-limited*; "The Ultimate Comp" in Delta Air Lines *SKY*; "The Biggest Game of the Year" in *Sport*; "The Mozart of the Poker Table" in *Poker World*; "Out of the Oscars, Into the Pan" was previously unpublished; all other stories originally appeared in *Cigar Aficionado*.

To Marvin Shanken and Gordon Mott,
who gambled on a writer and won.

Acknowledgements

Gordon Mott, Duncan Christy, John Birmingham, Bill Shapiro, Michael Caruso and Bob Roe, magazine editors of clear vision and exquisitely good taste. Deke Castleman, the kind of sublime manuscript editor every writer longs for. Lynne Loomis, the meticulous line editor. Anthony Curtis, the smart guy who made it happen. Corlan Chinn, a man who knows a hot story when he squeezes it. Pat Fleming, as fine a poker teacher as he is a poker player. And Renice and Eugene Konik, well-meaning parents who inadvertently encouraged in their inquisitive son an unseemly fascination with pool halls, casinos, and other dens of iniquity. To all: Thank you.

Table of Contents

Introduction

Many years ago, as a struggling freelancer in New York City, I dreamed of clawing my way out of writerly poverty. How, I wasn't sure. (My steady "job"—authoring "dirty letters" for porno magazines—certainly wouldn't do it.) Having failed to master the rudiments of obsequiousness and lacking the stomach to dutifully transcribe a press agent's brochure copy, I was ill-equipped to write fawning "profiles" of vapid celebrities or regurgitated brochure copy disguised as "travel stories." I wanted to file missives from the real world, a strange and glorious land that was just around the corner, but almost always overlooked.

One of my porno clients offered a juicy "men's magazine" assignment: Cover some big card-playing tournament called the World Series of Poker in downtown Las Vegas, and bring back stories of the courageous competitors who bet the average American's yearly salary on the fickle turn of a card.

I jumped at the chance. Not only were these gamblers the kind of larger-than-life characters that piqued my imagination, but poker had always fascinated me. Ever since high school, when I read and re-read a book called *Total Poker* by a British chap named David Spanier and played my buddies for quarters, I loved poker and fancied myself quite the sharpie. Here was an opportunity to write about the game *and* make a killing at the tables.

I lost all my money that first trip to Las Vegas.

I lost it three and four dollars at a time, playing in the smallest seven-card stud game in town. And if the machine that ate my bank card would have spit out more crisp hundred-dollar bills, I would have lost them, too.

The locals carved me up like fresh squab. "First time out here?" one of them asked. I was too ashamed to admit the truth.

Which was this: I was awestruck. I was astounded. I had never seen (nor imagined) a place like Las Vegas. When the cab from the airport took me down Fremont Street (this was in the days before it was converted to a pedestrian mall), through a corridor of lights that turned night to day, I actually *gasped*. Could a place this fantastical really exist?

Even more remarkable to me was the discovery that there were denizens of this neon universe that actually made a living playing games of chance. These were people who, for instance, played poker so well they won tournaments year after year. I watched these people closely. I had no choice. They were the very folks who were dashing my dream—the one that had me elevated from ink-stained wretch to suave gambler dude—on the green felt of the Horseshoe's poker tables. I scribbled down anecdotes about the top poker players. I observed their motions and their dress and the way they rubbed their eyes in the wee hours of the morning. I tried to know them.

It took me several years of visits to Las Vegas before I was able to beat the poker games, and several more before I knew how to win a poker tournament. But in that time my respect for—and curiosity about—the exalted few who had made successes of themselves in this seductive and cruel town grew like a hot progressive jackpot meter. How did they do it? What were their secrets? Why were they winners? Eventually, I learned some of the answers (which I gladly share with you in the forthcoming pages). Every revelation brought more questions, greater enigmas. Spending as much time hanging around casinos as I did, I came to know the bright lights and dark corners of this milieu—and the dice players and card counters and roulette junkies that inhabited this peculiar world.

I play poker a bit better these days. And the only "dirty letters" I write are to my lover. But I'm still fascinated by the winners and losers that make the casino—and everywhere else risk meets reward—such a colorful place.

Let me take you inside.

The Man With
the $100,000 Breasts

When I first meet Brian Zembic, he is living in a bathroom.

This is not because he can't afford a place that has all the amenities, like a bedroom. It's because a couple of his degenerate gambling buddies bet him $14,000 he couldn't stay in a bathroom for 30 straight days.

Several gambler friends playing the poker tournament circuit had told me about some psychopath they knew who would do anything to win a bet. "The guy's an animal," they opined. "You gotta meet him." But my pals neglected to mention that Brian doesn't really have a permanent address, save for a cheap motel he often stays in when he comes to Las Vegas. Tracking him down is like hunting a fugitive; he seems to jump to another motel, another apartment, another country, every time I try to get him on the phone. That he is confined to a bathroom for a month is my best opportunity yet to actually confirm this cipher's existence.

When I arrive in Las Vegas, he's six days into the bathroom bet, and already he's going a little stir-crazy. As far as bathrooms go, it's a nice bathroom: carpeted, brightly lighted, bordering on spacious. But it's still a bathroom. The terms of Brian's bet allow him to keep the door open, but prohibit him from crossing the threshold into the adjoining hallway. Since Brian lives in the bathroom by himself—a

$50-a-day housekeeper brings him sandwiches whenever he yells for her—most of his time is spent reading and practicing magic tricks. Rows of $100 bills are taped to the mirror to remind Brian what he's earning each day he serves his self-imposed sentence but, he confesses, his resolve is weakening. "Joey, one of the guys who made the wager with me, he owns the apartment and he's been sending people over here to take a dump," Brian tells me, reclining on the floor. "It's brutal."

Six days later his buddies cave in and buy Brian out of the bet for $7,000.

"I didn't think he'd do it, to tell you the truth," Joey admits, shortly after paying Brian off with a thick stack of hundreds. "I wouldn't do it. You wouldn't do it, right? I couldn't imagine myself or anybody else with half a brain staying in a bathroom for a month. I thought it was a good bet. I was wrong."

Anyone who knows Brian Zembic well understands the guy will do just about anything to put money in his pocket—as long as it doesn't require punching a clock. Ironically, Brian's a top Las Vegas blackjack player, one of the world's best at "shuffle tracking," a complex method of following cards through the mixing process. He could be earning thousands of dollars a day plying his trade. But he doesn't do it regularly because that would feel too much like *working*, a concept that Brian despises. Working, he believes, means somebody owns him, owns his time, his freedom. When he needs to earn some money, which happens occasionally, he gambles. Backgammon mostly, a little poker, ping-pong when he can find a sucker—anything where his skill gives him the edge. Anything where his superior talent or knowledge makes him a favorite to win. This includes taking insane proposition bets. Like walking around for a year with a nice pair of womanly breasts.

When I meet him at his bathroom prison cell that summer afternoon, he's had them for close to a year. He's wearing a baggy sweatshirt, so his bustiness isn't obvious. But you can tell there's something lurking under all that cotton. I ask Brian if the past 10 months have been humiliating. He laughs. "No. Not at all. It's been great. I've probably never had more fun in my life."

Fun? Playing with big beautiful breasts every day of the year I can see. But *possessing* them?

"Let me put it this way," Brian says, smiling conspiratorially, as his housekeeper shuffles past the doorway. "I've never gotten so much pussy in my life. I mean, I've never done bad. But since I got these," he says, giving his bosom an absentminded poke, "it's been like one woman after another."

* * *

For Brian Zembic, 37, from Winnipeg, Manitoba, life has not always been so busty. He's always been an attention-getter, a fast-talking high-energy maniac who usually reduces everyone around him to a chuckling mess. Even though he's notorious for never picking up a check—Brian's possibly the cheapest bastard on the planet—his buddies love taking him out to dinner and nightclubs, because he's a total chick magnet. Friends call him "the Wiz," short for Wizard. Brian's like a sorcerer. He does magic tricks and tells jokes and makes women you would be too scared to talk to giggle like teenagers at an Antonio Sabato Jr. underwear signing.

Brian the Wiz does not look like what you might imagine a hard-core gambler to look like. No gold chains. No pinkie rings. No dark sunglasses. He's got a boyish face and an easy grin. (And large breasts.) In terms of physique and looks and presence, you would probably call Brian average. Average height and weight. Average build. Nondescript. Indeed, a little more than a year ago, Brian was, like any other guy, flat-chested—and perfectly happy that way.

But one night a couple of years ago, Brian was playing backgammon at the Ace Point Club in New York City. It's a quasi-legal dingy little place in midtown Manhattan that looks like someone's living room, except that it's filled with backgammon tables and a cast of shady characters you probably wouldn't want hanging around if it were *your* living room. This is Brian's world. On this particular night he's playing for $300 a point with his high-rolling pals, a gang of action junkies escaped from the pages of a Damon Runyon story: magicians, card cheats, sports bettors. Guys who are prone to bet on which raindrop will get to the bottom of a window pane first. The conversations in this crowd tend toward the deeply philosophical.

"What would you play Russian Roulette for?"

"I dunno. A million, maybe."

"Yeah? How much for two bullets in the gun?"

Tonight, a cold desperate winter night in 1996, Brian is engaged in a passionate debate with his cohort JoBo, one of the biggest backgammon players on the planet. Like the stakes he plays for, JoBo is a large man, a stout man, a man with thick forearms and a powerful chest. He tends to express his opinions with a stolid certainty that does not invite contradiction. JoBo's saying it's crazy how women get implants, how, in hopes of attracting men, they actually jam a bag of saltwater in their chest.

Brian suggests that getting implants probably isn't so bad. "Look at Maggie," he says, referring to a mutual friend with a substantial breast job. "She seems pretty happy with her boobs."

"You think so?" JoBo asks. "How'd you like it if you had to walk around with those things all day?"

Brian leans back in his chair and laughs. JoBo is not a man who likes to be laughed at. He's the kind of guy who frequently challenges those who contradict him to put their money where their mouth is.

"Tell you what, pal," JoBo says. "I'll give you a hundred thousand if *you* get tits."

Now, a hundred grand to JoBo isn't going to change his life one way or another. He plays backgammon matches against Saudi sheiks for stakes nearly that big. So Brian knows JoBo isn't fooling. JoBo really *would* pay $100,000 just to see one of his friends sporting a set of perky breasts.

And $100,000 to Brian Zembic—$100,000 for not working—is a serious matter.

"How large would they have to be?" Brian asks.

"As big as Maggie's, of course."

They discuss the wager's fine points: Brian's responsible for the surgery costs; JoBo will put the $100,000 prize in escrow; Brian collects the money only if he keeps his breasts for a year.

"Okay," Brian says. "You're locked into it."

Sure, whatever. JoBo knows Brian is the kind of goofball who likes to talk a good game. It's part of his life-of-the-party shtick.

"And you know I'm fucked up enough to do it," Brian warns.

"No you're not," JoBo says. "Nobody's that fucked up."

For the next three months, JoBo and Brian play a lot of backgammon together. Every time they see a woman with attractive shapely breasts, they joke about their crazy bet.

After one long night of rolling the cubes, Brian confides in JoBo that he's going to put a lot of money in the stock market. Seems his pal Fat Steve, another Vegas wiseguy, has a can't-miss tip. "And if it does miss," Brian tells JoBo, "I figure I've got your hundred-thousand-dollar insurance policy."

During the summer of '96, Brian, on Steve's advice, buys stock in some company that makes heart-scanning equipment. Coincidentally, JoBo already owns a bunch of shares, and also assures him it's the stock of the century. So Brian plunges a huge chunk of his savings, a total of $125,000, into the deal. Meanwhile, JoBo's unloading his shares as quickly as his broker can find some sucker to buy them. In one week the stock goes from 6 1/2 to 5.

Brian finds out he's been duped by his buddy. He unleashes a vitriolic monologue at JoBo, alternately calling him a scumbag-cocksucking-ass-licking-motherfucker and hanging up on him. This is how Brian typically deals with anger: call, scream, swear, hang up. His friends know this. The bitterness passes and Brian goes back to being the Wiz.

This time, though, the ranting doesn't bring Brian any satisfaction. He's still steamed. So, a week after his stock debacle, pissed off and stuck, he threatens to get breasts.

"No," JoBo says, "you waited too long. Bet's off."

Brian disagrees. So the two gamblers do what most gamblers do when confronted with an intractable difference of opinion: They convene an arbitration panel of fellow gamblers—in this case, three allegedly impartial jurists who happen to be JoBo's high-rolling friends. These are fellows whose combined weight would probably eclipse that of the Packers' offensive line, guys who have mastered the art of consuming 6,000 calories a day while doing nothing but playing cards and backgammon and the occasional video game. They look like a trio of Buddhas.

In a big booth at a Chinese restaurant off the Vegas Strip, Brian and JoBo make their case before the panel, which has dubbed itself the Titty Tribunal. After five minutes of solemn deliberation, over plates of moo shu pork, Mongolian beef, and most everything else on the menu, the tribunal issues its ruling: The bet's on.

*　*　*

Brian's little joke is no longer a joke. He's got a deal. But now he's got to figure out how to hold up his end of it—if he truly *wants* to hold up his end. Any doubts he might harbor pass quickly, thanks to a profound analytical technique Brian often resorts to when confronted with tough decisions. "I don't think about things too much," he explains. "Once I make up my mind, it's over."

Brian knows a plastic surgeon, a scalpel-wielding casino junkie he and his cohorts sometimes gamble with. "Would you give me breast implants?" Brian asks the doctor. "In a heartbeat," Doc says. "I work on transsexuals all the time."

Thinking maybe his gambling doctor buddy isn't necessarily the most responsible member of the medical community—the guy spends at least half his waking hours playing backgammon—Brian seeks a second and third opinion. Every surgeon says yes. "Not one of them had a single ethical or legal or moral qualm," Brian recalls. "They were all, like, 'Sure, I'll give you tits!'"

Doc's fee is $4,000 to put them in, $500 to take them out. Now, Brian, being about the stingiest miser to ever roll a pair of dice, balks at the price. Oh, he has the money. He just doesn't want to spend 4.5% of his expected profit.

So Brian makes the surgeon a proposition. They'll play a little backgammon. A $5,000 match. Brian has the operation paid for in two hours.

Now Brian the Wiz realizes the surgery is really going to occur. That he's only hours away from going under the knife. That he's going to have *tits*. At this point, most men would be queasy at the thought of getting their nipples sliced open. But Doc assures him the operation isn't really out of the ordinary. Putting implants in a man, he says, is virtually no different than in a woman. Brian has nothing to worry about. A little nip, a little tuck—sew it up and out the door. Simple.

Sure, except for the two big mounds he's going to be carrying around for a year. After all, if our balls, our testosterone-filled testicles, are the nexus of our manhood, then breasts—protruding insistent mammaries—are surely one of the hallmarks of womanhood. But Brian is calm. Eerily calm.

You or I would be wondering and worrying, allowing visions of embarrassment and unwanted femininity and, God forbid, impotence, to dance in our muddled heads. What's going to happen when my poker buddies see me built like a centerfold? How am I going to explain this to the first woman I coax into bed? What the fuck is wrong with me?

That's why we're not the Wiz.

On a gray Manhattan winter afternoon, Brian Zembic has clear plastic pouches inserted through his nipples (over the pectoral muscles) and filled with 14 ounces of saline. After a routine two-hour procedure, he is the proud owner of two 38C breasts.

"I was in a serious motorcycle accident a few years ago," Brian says. "I went through fifteen different operations to put my body back together. Compared to having your jaw reconstructed and your skull held together by pins, getting a boob job is nothing."

He recalls feeling vaguely heavy—top-heavy—when he wakes. "Everything went smoothly," Brian says. "I just couldn't get out of bed for two weeks." He remembers being interminably groggy, with a chronically sore back. And a lingering fear of touching his new breasts.

"I was afraid of popping them," he says. "I thought if I touched them they might fall out."

Instead, Brian looks. He ogles his breasts, just as some guys might slather over a stripper. Most of the time that he's in bed, he keeps his tits hidden under a sweatshirt. But whenever he gets the urge, he takes a peek. And he's got to admit, they look pretty damn good. Finally, about two weeks after his surgery, after everything has "settled," Brian has his first squeeze.

His new breasts feel hard, as though the doctor implanted two regulation softballs. (Eventually they soften.) Every time he touches his breasts Brian wants to laugh— "I've got tits!" he's thinking—so he has to stop touching them. Laughing hurts his scars too much.

Men joke that if they had tits of their own, they could quit chasing women. Brian Zembic proves otherwise. "I was hoping it would be a turn-on to squeeze my tits," Brian admits. "But I never had much feeling in that area before the operation and I didn't have any afterward. I was a little disappointed."

Shortly after his initial grope, as soon as he's mobile, Brian calls his buddy JoBo. "For Christ sake, take 'em out! I was bluffing," JoBo says. "I didn't think you'd actually do it." JoBo offers to settle the bet for $50,000. Brian tells him the breasts are staying right where they are—he intends to collect his $100,000.

JoBo is sick. He thinks he might vomit. What sort of

twisted lunatic would actually go through with this? "You cheap, ugly, little cocksucker!" he screams. "You've got to be kidding me!"

Brian isn't kidding.

"Then I'm going to get my money's worth," JoBo vows. "Get your ass over to the club, you little prick. It's time for a show."

For his "debut," Brian briefly considers wearing the baggiest trench coat he can find. "But then I think, I should be proud of my tits," Brian says. "Not many guys would have the balls to walk around with a pair of hooters."

No, indeed they would not. You can grow a ponytail or wear an earring or, if you're really a "rebel," smear on some eye shadow. But how "different" does that make you from every other guy in the world seeking an anchor of individuality in a sea of matching ties and nicely creased Dockers? Brian has breasts, 38C breasts. *That's* different.

It's nearly midnight, but the Ace Point is still full of gamblers. When Brian appears at the backgammon club, dressed as he always dresses, in a T-shirt and bomber jacket, a small crowd forms at JoBo's beckoning. "You could tell some people were almost scared to look, like at a murder scene," Brian recalls. When he lifts his shirt to reveal two round protuberant mounds peeking over his hairy belly, JoBo laughs so hard he almost pukes. "You keep these for a year, and it'll be worth every penny."

Mikey Large, a regular at the high-stakes backgammon games, keeps begging Brian for another peek. He likes the breasts. A lot. Brian calls him a pervert, a sick twisted lowlife. And flashes him anyway. At this point, his breasts are a new toy, like a flashy watch or a graphite-shafted oversize driver: Hey, boys, look what I got!

"It was like seeing a beautiful long-haired girl from behind," JoBo recalls. "You're falling in love, and then she turns around and you see it's some rocker dude with a moustache. Most men find that disturbing. I found Brian's tits disturbing. But funny, too."

* * *

Proving to your buddies you have titanium testes is fine. Winning a $100,000 bet is fantastic. But no sex for a year? That's a torturous proposition. Initially Brian thinks that when he's around women he'll have to try to hide his breasts, that his year will be filled with ingenious subterfuges and concealments. He learns quickly that, dressed in baggy clothes and a jacket, almost no one can tell he's stacked. Within a few weeks, after sharing his secret with several female friends, it becomes clear to Brian that most women do not regard him as a nauseating freak. They *like* his breasts.

"I was getting 'chi-chi' three weeks after the surgery," Brian claims.

He says that having breasts forges a bond between him and womankind. "Women feel closer to me now. My female friends, we walk around topless together. We compare our cleavage and talk about bras, like I'm one of the girls."

His first post-operation lover is a jeweler from New York City. Brian meets her at a party, where he tells her about his unique accessories, demurely hidden under a loose-fitting jacket. She smiles and says matter-of-factly, "That arouses me. I want to see them." A half-hour later they're in her apartment.

"She attacked me!" Brian says, still in awe at the memory. "She wouldn't stop sucking on them."

This, according to Brian, is standard procedure. "A few of the girls I've met have been extremely turned on by them," he reports. "They want to suck on them and play with them. All the stuff guys like to do."

I ask Brian if *he's* grown to like his breasts. "I'm really a tit man. I'm totally fixated on breasts. Unfortunately," Brian Zembic says, jostling his boobs, "these don't turn me on. I wish they did, but they just don't. I guess I want all the other tits out there, not mine."

Most men, as JoBo asserts, find Brian's breasts rather

unattractive, if not downright weird. "I guess it's because they tend to have chest hair growing on them, even though I shave them once in a while," Brian says. "But the women! I'm telling you, I don't know if it's like a latent lesbian thing or what. Seriously, the chicks are nuts for them."

Incredulous, I track down a couple of the women Brian claims to have slept with. One of them, Jeannie, a leggy stripper who works at one of the topless joints off Las Vegas Boulevard, says she's bisexual, and that Brian and his breasts fulfill all her fantasies at once.

"It's just awesome to get fucked *and* have nice tits to suck on," Jeannie explains. I tell her I understand completely.

Sharon, a smashing redhead who might pass for Geena Davis—if only Geena Davis worked as a blackjack dealer at a major Vegas casino—is a woman Brian had pursued for months, to no avail. "I thought he was funny. Kind of silly and harmless," she says. "Well, one day he left me a little love note with a naked picture of him, with his boobs. I could hardly stop laughing. If you know him, you realize only Brian would do that."

Sharon initially resisted Brian's attributes. "At first I told him, 'Too bad, I'm not looking for a guy with tits.' But then I got curious."

Brian, for his part, has no regrets about taking up JoBo's bet. He hasn't sworn off gambling; he hasn't stopped carousing; he's not treated like a leprous outcast. "Everything is just like before. Only I can't jog." Fact is, most strangers can't tell that Brian Zembic has breasts. I meet him one afternoon at a casino coffee shop, where hundreds of tourists congregate for cheap steak and a sympathetic ear. Nobody notices Brian's bosom. Thanks to his unflattering ensemble—untucked sweatshirt, windbreaker—even I can't tell the Wiz is lugging around a set of bodacious ta-tas. It's only when he wants the world to know that his secret becomes a public spectacle.

What about his family? Can he keep his rack from them? Sure, but he doesn't have to. His family, back in

Canada, thinks his saline-pouch adventure is a big hoot. "It hasn't fazed them a bit," Brian says. "My brothers laugh their asses off." Brian hasn't talked to his mom in several years, but he has told his dad about the breasts, and his dad says, hell yeah, if someone gave him $100,000, he would do it too.

Of everyone who knows him, Brian insists, not one person disapproves of his decision. Some have been more shocked than others, but no one has condemned him for taking a silly joke too far. One day Brian walks into the cardroom at a Strip casino, where he encounters Herbie, an old friend who hasn't seen him in a few years. They've talked on the phone, and Brian has told his friend about getting the breasts. But Herbie thought the Wiz was joking. Like he always jokes. When Herbie sees Brian in the cardroom, he claps Brian on the back and says, "Hey, man, what's up?" Brian shrugs, pulls up his shirt, and says, "These."

Herbie freaks out a little. But only because he's surprised. He says, after calming down, that he actually likes Brian's breasts, though he wouldn't mind them slightly bigger.

"Guy's a pervert," Brian says.

Life with breasts is sweet. In fact, Brian Zembic insists he's already a richer man for his troubles—besides the money. "This has been very educational for me," Brian says. "I feel I understand women a lot better. Having breasts gives you insight. You see what life is like for women. Taking hours to dress, worrying about how your breasts look. And you start to see what pigs we men are, the way we talk about breasts, like they're jewelry or a hat or something." The Wiz doesn't use words like *objectification*, but he knows now how it feels to have a part of your body talked about as though it weren't a part of you.

* * *

Brian and I are at Joey's apartment in Vegas, down the street from the Desert Inn. The Wiz is showing me some

16

sleight-of-hand magic tricks. He's astoundingly good at them. But my mind keeps wandering.

In the interest of investigative journalism—and because I'm going insane with curiosity—I ask Brian if I can feel his breasts. "Oh, man!" he says, grimacing. "Do you have to?" I tell him I do.

He sighs heavily. Most guys don't ask for a squeeze, because they're afraid the Wiz will think they're a fag or a pervert. He giggles nervously, like a teenaged girl letting her high-school boyfriend get his first grope. These are his tits, for God's sake!

Brian lifts his T-shirt and peels up his sports bra. There they are: breasts, round and womanly and appealing. I reach over and give the breast closest to me a perfunctory squeeze. It feels pretty good, almost natural. I'm thinking I might even enjoy a breast such as this, if only it didn't have razor stubble all over it. "Not bad," I say, relieved to have discharged my reportorial duties without any messy psychosexual complications.

Brian seems pleased. Maybe even proud. He knows these implants aren't really an organic part of him. They're a synthetic miracle concocted by a plastics company, and temporarily joined to him because of a $100,000 bet. He knows one day soon they'll be gone, disposed of in a medical waste bin. Still, Brian, you can tell, is far from ashamed of his breasts; he's got pride in them as though they were pretty eyes or graceful hands or sculpted abs. They are the crowning feature that makes him unique, that completes the legend of the Wiz. One day I'm talking with him on the phone, and I jokingly refer to his breasts as "those ugly-ass tits." He hangs up on me.

This is when I start to suspect that Brian Zembic, Mr. Do Anything For a Bet, isn't counting the minutes until he can lose his breasts and find another wager to conquer. He's had them nearly a year, but I haven't heard any impending plans for surgical reversal. So when I see him next a few weeks later back in Vegas, at the Mirage, where he's ensconced in a poker game, I ask him, "Are you going to get your tits removed when time's up?"

He smiles bashfully. "I thought I would. I mean, I *know* I will eventually," Brian says, adjusting his bra. "But to tell you the truth, I'm in no hurry to lose them." He exchanges grins with a long-legged cocktail waitress passing by. "No hurry at all."

*   *   *

A month later, late in 1997, Brian is in Monte Carlo, playing in a monster backgammon match. JoBo's there, too. So is Joey. They're all sharing a hotel suite, chasing down "chi-chi" and running up a $10,000 room-service bill.

Over the phone I ask the boys if they've come up with another can't-miss wager to enliven their time on the continent. Riding a unicycle in the nude, perhaps. "No," JoBo snarls. "I've learned my lesson. I won't make any more stupid bets with that cheap, ugly motherfucker."

And thus the one-year deadline comes and goes. The Wiz wins.

Brian gets his money, deposited into a Swiss bank account. The chi-chi flows freely. And still the ersatz breasts remain firmly implanted in his hairy chest.

They're still there, 18 months after he had his $100,000 operation.

Brian is chronically lazy. He admits it. But sloth doesn't explain why he doesn't have—why to this day he hasn't had—his breasts removed. Why he doesn't return to his former life as a decidedly flat-chested cleavage-less man.

"I don't know. It's kind of fun to have them," Brian mumbles over the international phone line.

He won't admit it: He *loves* his breasts. He loves that he's the only guy currently walking the Earth who has the nerve to do what he has done. He loves that he's the Wiz. And nobody will ever forget him.

"Who knows, maybe I'll keep them for another three months," he equivocates. "Maybe I'll keep them for six months, a year. I don't know. I don't want to do the operation over here. I'll probably wait until I get home. You know, I'm thinking of using the money to buy a house—no more stock market. I might buy a place in Vegas, or maybe Montreal. Maybe I'll buy something here in Europe. I don't know."

I reckon Brian Zembic might never have his breasts removed. Maybe he thinks he's starting a trend. Maybe he thinks history will remember him as an innovator, the guy who brought new and unimagined meaning to the phrase "tit man." I try to get the Wiz to give me a straight answer, to tell me when exactly he's going to face the scalpel and lose the breasts.

But he says he can't stay on the phone any longer. He's got to run. Seems there's this hot 19-year-old he met on the beach who's crazy for his tits, and he's got to meet her for dinner, where, if all goes as planned, she'll give him a hand job in the restaurant.

"And she better do it!" Brian the Wiz says. "I bet JoBo a thousand she would."

In the Casino

2

The Cold-Deck Crew

In the long run, after thousands of hands of baccarat, millions of pulls on the slot machines, and dozens of complimentary drinks, nearly everyone who plays casino games on the square loses. That's the way the gaming industry works: The house has the edge; the house gets the money.

Unless you're an expert player, there are but two ways to consistently beat the casinos: get enormously lucky, or cheat. The average gambler makes his bet and hopes for the improbable; sophisticated hustlers help themselves.

In fact, according to many gaming experts, it's nearly impossible to quantify how much money crews of skilled casino cheaters steal every year, though $50 million, they say, would not be an unreasonable figure. "We spend a hell of a lot of money trying to catch these crooks," says the head of security at a prominent downtown Las Vegas casino. "And every time we come up with a new technology to prevent large-scale cheating, the thieves seem to come up with a way to bypass it. It's a never-ending cat-and-mouse game."

"Dice mobs," who switch loaded or mis-spotted dice into casino crap games, can grind out thousands of dollars a day. "Slot crews," who prey on unwatched machines, employ expert locksmiths capable of breaking into vulnerable coin banks. And gangs of "muckers," sleight-of-hand artists who can "hold out" extra cards in the palm of their hand and take them in and out of casino games at will, can make a blackjack hand of virtually any total.

One notorious syndicate, led by a well-known organized crime figure, is believed to have netted more than $80 million before being ratted out by an accomplice who feared he was about to be murdered. Like serial bank robbers, thanks to Orwellian surveillance cameras and dishonor among thieves, the cheaters are almost always discovered and sent to prison.

Except one team.

The most ingenious crew ever to work the American casino circuit stole more than $3 million a year for five years—and never got caught.

Their story hasn't been told before. But now that one of the most accomplished gang of swindlers in the history of the larceny business is "in retirement," its members either dead, gainfully employed in the upper echelons of respectable corporations, or relocated to tropical islands, their ringleader is willing to reveal how he and his crew of grifters pulled off one of the greatest scams in casino history.

* * *

Among crossroaders (a subculture of con men, liars, and cheats descended from the crooked riverboat gamblers immortalized in Twain's *Life on the Mississippi*, secretive men— and a handful of women—who play everything from carnival games to three-card monte to bar dice), Robert "Mickey" Swift is a legend. In several decades of hustling he's amassed an encyclopedic compendium of swindling knowledge—perhaps nobody in the world knows more about cheating than Mickey Swift—and a small fortune in misbegotten gains. From humble, even squalid, roots in the Depression-era rural South, Mickey Swift traveled across the country with a crew of scrappy old-timers, learning a thousand deceitful ways to separate a mark from his money. He was taught how to play backgammon with "juiced"

24

(magnetic) dice, how to work a deck of "strippers" (cards with irregularly shaved sides), how to hold out the aces, how to execute a false shuffle, and how to mark cards with everything from petroleum jelly to nose perspiration. It took many hard years of itinerant grifting, but Mickey Swift eventually grew from a small-time "nit" to a master of chicanery.

He settled in Las Vegas in the early 1970s. "Back then it had a frontier-town feel," he recalls in a hushed drawl that belies his heart-of-the-Confederacy upbringing. "It wasn't a city filled with resorts and volcanoes and kiddie rides. But one thing has always been the same: There's always been plenty of money here, plenty worth going after."

In the early years Swift pulled a variety of scams, pocketing close to $100,000 annually. "The money was good, of course," Swift recalls. "But the thrill was what kept me going. There's nothing quite so exciting as the charge you get out of outsmarting the house. We didn't steal from tourists; in fact, most gamblers wouldn't even know what was going on if they saw a play happening. We went after the corporations, the casinos. Making money is fine. But making it through larceny is even better. I think everybody likes the feeling of getting away with something."

One of his favorite schemes involved switching "tops," mis-spotted dice, on and off Vegas crap tables. When the stickman offered Mickey the casino's dice, he would pick them up and in one deft motion replace them with his own homemade version (complete with imitation logo and serial number) concealed in his palm. The dice looked and felt legitimate, but they had spots representing only three numbers printed on them: two, three, and six, a combination that made rolling a losing 7 impossible. Whenever Mickey shot his tops, a confederate at the other end of the table would load up big bets on the numbers. After a lucrative pass or two, Swift, employing his graceful sleight-of-hand artistry, would switch the casino's dice back into the game. "Your heart tends to pound a bit when you make the move—you drop the extra dice and you're dead. But I've had a little practice," he says wryly.

In Reno he "put down paper," introducing "shaded" (marked) cards into blackjack games. "It was like playing with the cards face up," he says, smiling coyly. In Las Vegas he got hired at a major Strip casino as a roulette dealer and allowed his agents to "past-post" the winning numbers. Then, when Atlantic City casinos opened in the 1970s, he worked with a gang of engineering experts 30 years his junior, known as the Computer Crew, who played blackjack with the aid of a miniature processor concealed inside the tip of a cowboy boot. As each card hit the table, Mickey would input its value using his big toe to click a solenoid. The computer could accurately predict what cards remained and would send an electronic message through a concealed wire leading to a tiny earpiece, directing Mickey to the proper play. "Jersey didn't have an electronic device law anyway, so it wasn't technically a cheat," Swift recalls, "but, yes, we did play with a pretty big edge."

Electronic technology combined with Swift's sleight-of-hand acumen proved a powerful combination. Using zoom cameras hidden in a lady's pocketbook and law-enforcement-style transceivers with inter-canal hearing aids taped inside of wigs, Swift and his team of college boys were able to "peek" the dealer's hole card. "It was easy, really. We'd have our girl parked at a slot machine, and we'd tell her, 'A little to your left. Up a little more. Down one inch. Got it! Hold your position.' We'd get a perfect picture of the dealer's card on videotape, run it back at slow motion, and learn the value." Determining the card on a video monitor inside a parked van, a confederate relayed the information back to the table via audio-link. Knowing the dealer's total, Swift and his crew gained a 6% advantage, triple the edge obtained by the world's most expert card counters.

"Playing with cameras and radios and computers opened a whole new world to me," Swift recalls. "Old-timers like me were used to getting by on our wits. We had to be good with the hands; we had to have some imagination and skill. I know grifters who would practice the pull-through shuffle 200 hours before they got it right." Swift grabs a deck of cards and demonstrates. "You actually riffle the cards," he says, giving them what looks to be a genuine mix. "But then when you box the two halves together," he says, squaring up the deck, "you pull the halves right through the back. Looks like a legit shuffle, doesn't it? Well, sit in front of a mirror for a couple months and you can do it, too."

He shakes his head. "Those kind of skills are vanishing. A few years ago I saw these young guys coming into the racket with computers and cameras and it made my pair of tops look like they belonged in a museum."

Swift, however, was not obsolete. The "young guys," an educated breed of sharpies raised on mathematics and *Mission Impossible,* revered him and his astonishing talent. There are maybe two or three people in the world who can handle a deck of cards as well as Mickey Swift. Hand him a freshly shuffled and cut deck of cards, he'll deal you four aces. Put those aces in random spots in the middle of the deck, he'll deal you four aces. Deal him any four random cards, he'll show you four aces. The man's hands are legendary.

Combined with their electronic hardware, the Computer Crew knew Mickey Swift's hands could net them a quarter-million dollars—in 10 minutes.

They rehearsed the play for three weeks in Laughlin, a casino town on the Colorado River at the southern tip of Nevada, working out the kinks, getting the timing right, betting $5 chips. When the 12-member crew was certain their move was undetectable from all angles, when every member of the team knew the play's choreography like a cornerback knows his pass coverage, they took the show to the big time, Las Vegas.

* * *

At a major Las Vegas Strip casino, around two on a Wednesday morning, when the cacophony of a thousand slot machines has dwindled to a lonely tinkling and the highest roller in the joint is betting a few black chips per hand, four crew members sit down at a $5 blackjack table. Their choice is no accident; having staked out the casino in advance, they know that in this pit one surveillance camera covers two tables—a lens is not permanently fixed on their target table. Within 20 minutes they've locked up all seven betting spots, monopolizing the game. Playing the eight-deck shoe on the square, betting the minimum on every hand, the "seat-stuffers" lose a few bucks but have a grand time doing it, joking with the pit boss, tipping the dealer generously, and generally behaving like a quartet of friendly tourists. The casino is glad to have them.

As the four shills dribble away their chips, another player, the "stud," moves into a seat on the other side of the pit, directly across from the targeted table. (The stud's dealer and the target table's dealer stand back-to-back.) He's tanned and muscular; the female dealer finds him charming and flirtatious. The pit boss, a chain-smoking ogre in a bad suit, takes a look at the stud and smirks. The boss has seen this type before: a guy more interested in getting laid than winning money. The casino is glad to have him.

Two "big shots," one of whom has a pricey-looking escort on his arm and one of whom is Mickey Swift, float through the casino, pausing occasionally to make a table-limit bet. In the process of getting "built in," they splash a few thousand on craps, blanket the roulette layout with $100 chips, and most tellingly, stuff their pockets with dozens of high-priced, long-shot keno tickets. The casino is exceptionally glad to have them.

As the big shots spread their money around, ensuring that the security cameras follow their every move, a new dealer comes on to the target table. Like every other dealer in the casino, he just wants to make it through his shift, collect a few tips, and go home. Unlike every other dealer in the casino, he's been exhaustively trained by Mickey Swift.

As the dealer moves into position, a drunk, sipping a

bottle of beer, stands at a nearby slot machine, blearily chasing a few quarters. Though he'll probably be busted in a few minutes, the casino is more or less glad to have him, too.

When the dealer comes to the end of the shoe, he announces to the pit boss, "Shuffle!" The pit boss, fantasizing what he would do with a busty escort like the one with the big shot, absentmindedly calls out, "Go ahead!" and takes a pull on his Marlboro. The dealer executes a legitimate shuffle, dividing the eight decks into two piles of approximately 200 cards, grabbing a chunk from each pile and mixing them together. When he's done, he offers the cards for a cut. The pit boss, dreaming about blondes in low-cut black dresses, takes a cursory glance at the table and checks his watch.

When the dealer begins to distribute the cards, the drunk wanders over to the target table, apparently a harmless spectator more concerned with nursing his beer than watching the game. But in fact, as each card hits the table, the drunk whispers its value into his "bottle," which has been rigged with a miniature radio transmitter.

A few hundred yards away, in the casino parking lot, a confederate they call "the Brain" begins inputting the numbers into a specially programmed computer.

The stud continues to play and flirt and lose. The big shots continue to play and yell and lose. The shills continue to play and joke and lose. These are the wee hours on the Vegas Strip, and business seems to be churning on as usual.

When the dealer has used up approximately half the cards in the shoe—about four decks—he gives the office to the drunk, who says, "End," into his bottle and wanders off into the night.

As the dealer places the cards into the discard rack, a rectangular plastic case to his right, he inserts a tiny knot of rubber band that's been wedged under a fingernail, called a "lug," on top of the stack. This little pebble of latex will create an infinitesimal break or "brief" in the stack of cards, marking the exact spot where the crew's information stops.

It's invisible to the security cameras, but to a trained grifter it denotes the beginning of a "slug" as clearly as a 30-foot marquee advertising the surf-and-turf special.

Now the crew goes into the four-corner offense, slowing the game down. They ask for change. They pause before requesting a hit. They consult the pit boss for advice on how to play a pair of eights. They buy the Brain time to crunch the numbers through his computer.

Minutes later, a runner meets the escort in the ladies room, where she receives a $100 bill that has the Brain's computer-generated "answers" scribbled on it, numbers like 51, 50, and 42. These numbers instruct the players to play five spots and take one hit; play five spots and take no hits; play four spots and take two hits; and so on.

Given the sequence of cards that has just been played at the target table, the Brain's computer has derived an optimal playing strategy that will bust the dealer virtually every hand.

* * *

The dealer comes to the end of the shoe. As he collects and pays off the final bets, the big shots split up, taking seats at the two blackjack tables on either side of the target table. They each plunk down large cash bets, in this case, $1,000. The surveillance cameras on either side of the target table zoom in on the big-money action like Patriot missiles, leaving the middle table unwatched. The pit boss snaps out of his reverie and takes a step closer to one of the big-money tables.

The dealer at the target table calls out, "Shuffle!" Without looking away from one of the big shot's $1,000 bet, the pit boss says, "Go ahead."

At that moment, the stud starts shoving an accomplice, who, on cue, has started a fictitious argument. They swear and yell and push at each other to the brink of punches. All eyes in the pit, including the boss', turn to him. With neither spectators nor supervision, the dealer at the target table splits his cards at the lug mark, divides the decks into two stacks, and proceeds to shuffle.

But the cards never change place.

As taught by Mickey Swift, the greatest card manipulator in the business, the dealer executes a "zero shuffle," a blatantly false mixing action similar to the "pull-through." But when it's viewed from the security cameras above, the shuffle looks like the real thing.

As the dealer squares the cards back to their original, predetermined order, the stud decides to settle his argument outside. Simultaneously, the escort approaches the pit boss and asks for some complimentary champagne to be sent to her table. The boss gives her a yellow grin and happily obliges. Without letting his eyes leave the escort's alluring backside as she sashays to her table, the pit boss says to the big shots, "Okay, good luck, fellas."

One of the shills cuts to a "crimp," a small, signatory bend between two cards, bringing the computer-analyzed "cooler" (prearranged sequence of cards) to the top of the shoe.

At that moment, the seat stuffers decide they've had enough. They cash in their chips, sheepishly ask for a comp to the coffee shop, and say goodnight.

On cue, the big shots move in from the neighboring tables.

"How you guys doing tonight?" the pit boss asks, flashing them a fraudulent smile.

"Hell, I'm down about twenty grand," Mickey Swift lies. "I'm leaving town in the morning and I'd love just to get even." He fishes a handful of $500 chips from his sport jacket and plunks them down on the first betting spot. "Whadda you say? Think we can get the table limit raised here? Maybe, I don't know, five thousand a hand?"

"Let me see what I can do," the pit boss says. He calls upstairs. Security tells him these two suckers have been walking around the casino all night littering the place with money. The shift manager gives the green light—he's thrilled to have their action. "Besides," the pit boss whispers into the phone, "they're coming in on a fresh shoe, so they're definitely not card counters. Let's fade 'em." He turns to the big shots. "Okay, gentlemen. You got it."

Based on where the escort rests her hand on the big shot's shoulder, he and Swift know how many spots to bet and how many hits to take. On the first round they make five $5,000 bets and take one card. "Boy, my heart's pounding now," Swift announces.

The dealer busts.

Then they make three $5,000 bets and take no cards. The dealer busts. They make six $5,000 bets and take two cards. The dealer busts.

In three minutes they're up over $70,000.

"I better stop," Mickey Swift tells the pit boss, who tries vainly to maintain a facade of friendliness. "This is unbelievable luck! Unbelievable!"

The pit boss, still certain he's got a couple of fish on the hook, doesn't want to lose their business, especially before they give back some of their "lucky" chips. "We'd love to have you stay," the boss says. "Is there anything I can do for you? Dinner? Are you staying here? I could get you our nicest suite."

"Nah, we better just go," Swift says.

"Are you sure?" the boss says, almost pleading.

"Well, okay. A few more hands. We'll play until we lose two hands in a row," Swift says, knowing that won't be for a while.

More than 50 hands and $200,000 later, the escort signals to Swift that the crew has come to the end of their computer cooler. "Tell you what," Swift says to his big-shot buddy, "let's play until we lose a hand." They gamble three hands on the square before finding a loser.

"Thanks," Mickey Swift says to the pit boss, pushing in a mountain of chips, nearly $250,000. "That was fun."

The boss nearly chokes on his words. "Thank you, gentlemen. Remember, if you care to stay, we're very glad to have you."

"You know what?" Swift says. "We're very glad to be here."

3

A Lot of Crap

The green felt is blanketed with $50,000 worth of multi-colored chips. These tokens, these silly little discs, belong to a huddle of 12 anxious people, none of whom have ever met. But like soldiers on the brink of combat, they share an unspoken bond, an unwavering devotion and fealty to two small red cubes with dots on all six sides.

The auto paint supplier from Cleveland has only a few hundred riding on the next roll; the real-estate broker to his left is gambling several thousand. But you can't tell who has the most at stake by looking at their faces: Everyone at this Caesars Palace crap table has adopted the expectant, aroused, slightly pained visage of a dice player awaiting the next fling of the bones. Oblivious to the Centurions and Roman goddesses posing for snapshots and Athenian maidens strolling past with trays of cocktails, thoroughly uninterested in the horse races and baseball games beamed into the adjacent sports book, these people are fixated on one man, an elderly fellow at the end of the table. The guy holding the dice.

Some of the bettors slump on their forearms, feigning nonchalance; some fiddle with their chips, compulsively arranging them into color-coordinated rows; some look as though they're praying.

The dealers try not to look bored. The box man, sitting

at the center of the table, surveys the layout like a human radar dish. The pit boss, vaguely interested, stands in the background with his arms crossed over his ill-fitting suit. For a moment—a moment that lasts two seconds—the congregation feels as though the cosmos revolves around this slab of wood, this emerald plane in the Nevada desert.

And a moment later all the denizens of Caesars Palace, briefly distracted from their own private dramas, look up and smile. Because an instant after the elderly fellow flings the dice, a startling joyous noise is heard echoing throughout Caesars' empire. It's the sound of someone beating the odds. Twelve strangers have made their point.

* * *

Of all the casino games, craps holds a special place in the hierarchy of American gambling. Before Ed Thorp wrote *Beat the Dealer* in 1962, transforming blackjack into the most popular pit game in the world, craps easily was the casino king. From Damon Runyon's dice-shooting hoods to Robert Redford in *Indecent Proposal*, craps has always attracted some of the most interesting characters in the casino—and certainly the loudest. Blackjack has its counters, baccarat its James Bond pretenders, and roulette its wheel-obsessed number watchers. Those who roll the bones, however, are a different breed, an amalgam of the bookish scholar and the degenerate gambler, thoughtful yet aggressive, cautious yet headstrong, a short-term winner and a long-term loser. Give a linebacker a bankroll and an advanced degree in probability and you might have the perfect diceman.

At the crap table you'll recognize everyone from the vaunted "high roller" (the dice game is where this now-generic term originated) to the tight-fisted "numbers man" with a proven "system." Offering a low minimum bet—a buck or two at many Las Vegas joints—craps is the most democratic of gambles, attracting both ends of the monetary spectrum. No matter their finances, players at the crap table are there for more or less the same reason: It's the only game in the casino where, without any special skills or expertise, the gambler can reduce the house edge to almost zero. And it is the game where miracles can happen. Very quickly.

Even where they deal the best rules, craps is still a negative-expectation proposition. So the surest way not to lose at the dice table is not to play. But what fun is that? For every sophisticate who wouldn't dream of risking his money at a crap game, there's someone with the dice in his hand recalling a story about the lucky sap whose pass-line prowess won the house, and the car, and the boat, and everything else.

* * *

Anyone who spends more time in a casino than he ought to can tell you a crap story or two. A handful of them won't be apocryphal.

The fanciful tales are legion:

"I saw a guy once. He turned five bucks into fifty-thousand dollars in twenty minutes. I'm serious!"

"There was this rich guy, right? He's betting, like, a hundred grand a roll."

"I didn't see it personally, but I heard there was this guy who bet a quarter-million on one roll, and he had a heart attack while the dice were in the air."

Some of the best (that is, true) stories emanate from Binion's Horseshoe in downtown Las Vegas. During the three weeks in spring that the Horseshoe hosts the World Series of Poker, the casino becomes the center of the poker universe. But during the rest of the year, Binion's flourishes on the strength of one remarkable distinction: It offers the world's highest limits.

In *Indecent Proposal*, Redford bets $1 million on the pass line, catches a winner, and invests the proceeds in a night of fun with Demi Moore. Impossible, right? The stuff of Hollywood?

Yes and no. In the movie, the gambling sequences take place at the Las Vegas Hilton. "It couldn't happen here," according to Jerry, a long-time Hilton pit boss. "We'd let him bet maybe a hundred grand. We don't need any more action than that."

Indeed, at most of Las Vegas' swanky uptown resorts— Bally's, Caesars Palace, the Mirage (all owned by large corporations)—relatively low betting limits lessen the house's exposure to inordinate fluctuations in the quarterly balance sheet. But down on Fremont Street, the famed Glitter Gulch of countless television shows and movies, the game is altogether different. At Binion's Horseshoe, not only could the $1 million bet happen, it did.

In 1985, a man named Robert Bergstrom, from Austin, Texas, called the Horseshoe's president, Jack Binion, on the phone. Bergstrom, who apparently possessed more money than sense, had recently lost $50,000 at the crap table. Thanks to a lucrative real-estate business, his plunge didn't keep him up at nights. In fact, Bergstrom was calling to ask whether he could return soon to bet a "significant amount." Jack Binion, adhering to his casino's policy of "your first bet is your limit, no matter how high," naturally said yes.

And that was the last he heard of the mysterious Texan. Until three months later.

"The guy calls up," Binion remembers, "and he says he's going to be here soon to make a very large bet. A couple nights later he shows up with two little suitcases, filled with exactly seven-hundred, seventy-seven thousand dollars. And he says he wants to bet it all."

Binion approved the bet: $777,000 on the pass line.

"I think it was a little old lady who was shooting the dice at the time," Binion recalls. "She made a point of nine, rolled maybe one or two numbers, a six and an eight, I think. And then another nine."

Bergstrom was a $777,000 winner.

He promptly collected his plunder, jumped into a beat-up old car, and left town. "I wanted to win that bet, sure," Binion says. "But we accept our losses. It's all part of the business. The losses definitely happen sometimes, especially when you're talking about a single bet, where we have very little edge. It's like flipping a coin. But, no, I didn't really mind losing that bet. Besides, I *want* to meet a guy who's capable of betting half a million or more on one roll."

Bergstrom, in fact, came back a few weeks later and bet $548,000 on the pass line. Again, an elderly woman shot the dice. Seconds later, this highest of rollers had 548 more $1,000 chips stacked before him.

Shortly thereafter, Bergstrom made his final trip to the Horseshoe. "I'm going to double or dump it," Binion recalls him saying, just before the Texan bet exactly $1 million on the pass line.

Once more, a geriatric lady rolled the dice, while an enormous audience vied to witness the results. Her first roll established the point, a 9 again—a 3-2 underdog for the player—and her second roll came up six-ace. A loser 7.

Bergstrom was never seen again.

While extraordinary, such prodigious bets are not entirely uncommon at Binion's Horseshoe. An octogenarian former jockey known as Fast Eddie has on four separate occasions run $100 up to more than $250,000. The poker manager at the Horseshoe, Jim Albrecht, says, "Eddie normally plays poker in the smallest game we offer: one- to four-dollar seven-card stud. He's basically a pensioner, living off Social Security. But that's craps for you. In a very short time, a few hours, Eddie has parlayed a handful of chips from his poker winnings into over a million dollars."

One time Fast Eddie set aside enough of his profits to purchase a new condo. The other three times he played on, and graciously gave the casino back all its money.

"The game goes so damned fast," Jack Binion comments. "It's like a pyramid, the way the money piles up. There's no other game where so much money can be won so fast. It's nothing unusual to take ten dollars and multiply it into five hundred, a thousand in a few minutes. And that's very exciting."

The way most dice players make a fortune is by catching what math mavens call a "favorable deviation from the norm." This means that in an infinite string of random numbers, a certain pre-ordained quantity of sevens, elevens, and other numbers will be rolled, approximately as many losers as winners. If you're fortunate enough to make your bets during a period of heavy clustering of winning numbers—otherwise known as a "hot streak"—the results can be sublimely gratifying. If you have the heart (some would say "ignorance") to press your bets with each winning roll, the results can be staggering. And if you happen to be playing during a once- or twice-in-a-lifetime situation—like an hour-long roll without a loser—your retirement will be quite comfortable.

Howard Schwartz, who runs the Gambler's Book Club in Las Vegas, which sells books that tell you everything you want (and don't want) to know about the game, says, "As the years go on and long stories grow longer, the money won and the number of passes the shooter made seem to grow as memories fade." No one is really sure of the longest string of passes—Binion seems to remember someone rolling 37 winners in a row at the Shoe—but according to Frank Scoblete, a prolific gambling author who writes widely on unbeatable games, Hawaiian Stanley Fujitake, known as the Golden Arm, made close to 50 passes at the California Casino in Las Vegas. "He held the dice for over three hours. It was a magnificent epic roll."

While there's no substitute for dumb luck, some eccentric crap shooters believe in "PK," psychokinesis, or mind over matter. Hard evidence of such powers is rarer than a clock on the casino floor.

Of course, the surest way to roll a desired number is to use doctored or loaded dice. Years ago, gangs of dice cheats could successfully introduce phony cubes into the game without detection. But modern surveillance and security techniques have made this kind of chicanery rare, if not extinct.

Betting "systems," due to the immutable laws of mathematics, cannot overcome the house advantage. Neither can talking to the dice, employing lucky talismans, or honoring ancient superstitions. For instance, many players call their bets "off" when one of the dice has been rolled off the table. They imagine that somehow the cube has "cooled" by hitting the casino floor. Others increase their wagers when a woman is rolling the bones, luck being a lady and all.

And then there are the utter fools. An Arab gentleman at the Riviera was fond of betting $1,000 a throw on the "big 6," a proposition bet that pays even money on a true 6-5 proposition. In effect, on every roll of the dice this fellow was handing the casino $91. (If he was committed to betting the number six, he could have "placed" the bet with the dealer, and got paid 7-6.) Anyone who has played craps for more than 10 minutes knows that of all the bets you mustn't ever take, the "big 6" is one of the worst offenders. It's a classic sucker bet.

Anyone who has played craps for more than 10 minutes also knows you don't tell another player how to spend his money. But the hard-bitten dice players gathered around the Arab's table couldn't stand to watch the carnage. "I can't take it," said a seasoned crap player named Bob. "It's your money and you can do what you want with it. But do you know you could be saving yourself over seven percent a roll by having the house place the six for you?" he politely asked the Arab.

Replied the Arab, "Of course, I am perfectly aware of this. But I would rather take the disadvantage than have someone else touch my chips."

Better odds aren't everything to some gamblers. Some people crave atmosphere over value. (These are the folks who keep the light bills paid and the faux volcano spewing.) This explains why many players settle for the paltry double odds offered at the carpet joints on the Strip, when several casinos around Las Vegas regularly deal games with 10x, 20x, and even 100x odds—resulting in a house advantage so small that, were every player to play in this fashion, the casino wouldn't earn enough to cover its overhead.

The way each casino handles its games—and the giant swings in fortune that accompany them—is a reflection of how they do business on a larger scale, especially when the high rollers hit town. One prominent New York City businessman is a favorite customer of a well-known Las Vegas casino. (For the sake of their reputations, both shall remain anonymous.) This New Yorker often charters a jet to Nevada, where he entertains friends and colleagues in a lavish courtesy suite and gambles more than any sane person should.

One week, the New Yorker flew to Vegas to play craps. He had established a line of credit well into the millions at a top casino, though he secretly had no intention of losing that much. After a week of rolling the bones, calling out combination bets, and riding out the inevitable hot and cold streaks, the New Yorker counted up his credit vouchers and realized he was down close to $600,000. Though he'd never admit it to anyone, least of all the casino, this was more than he could afford to lose. He was so distraught he didn't even bother to avail himself of the casino's complimentary limousine: Like a true New Yorker, he hopped a cab to the airport.

Now this abrupt decision caused some concern at the casino's front offices. The casino loves customers like the New Yorker. It *adores* them. For as sure as rolling a 7 is a 2-1 favorite over rolling a 10, a dedicated, well-financed crap player will, over time, make the casino very rich. To the casino bosses, a customer like the New Yorker is a trophy fish on the hook—and they're willing to do almost anything to reel him back to their boat.

A limousine was dispatched to retrieve the departing mark. That this limo happened to be filled with champagne, caviar, and two phenomenally expensive call girls would, the casino hoped, impress upon the New Yorker the special place he occupied in the casino's heart. At the airport, the professional companions approached the gambler and delivered a message: "We want you to come back. Anything you want for the rest of your stay you can have. Including us."

The New Yorker went back.

Three days later, after much imbibing, carousing, and

yes, crap shooting, the New York City businessman returned to the airport—with $3 million of dice-begotten profit.

"It's a wonderful game, this craps," he was heard to say. "A wonderful game."

4

Count On It!

Nothing draws money to a casino's gambling pits like Fight Night. Nothing. Not the lure of stretch limousines or gourmet meals. Not fawning employees or enormous suites the size of a suburban house. Not even private yachts or chartered jets.

Fight Night is where everyone who fancies himself a casino VIP discovers just how "VI" of a "P" he really is. This particular Fight Night is headquartered at Caesars Palace, one of Las Vegas' premier shrines to unbridled opulence. Hours before a lunatic hang-glider crashes into the ring ropes during the main event, you can sense this will be a memorable evening. Even the dealers, who normally look about as enthusiastic as toll collectors, stand expectantly over empty roulette wheels and bare baccarat tables. Tonight they look like budding actors anxiously awaiting their first entrance onto a summer-stock stage.

Fight Night attracts big money from Europe, the Middle East, the Orient. The "whales," as they're known in the business, will swim in from Dallas and Chicago and Miami, too. Every corner of the planet will be well represented tonight. Prosperity suffuses the air like perfume at the duty-free counter of an international airport. Big bettors mean big tips. Tended to correctly, a roomful of heavy hitters spreads around $100 gratuities the way a bougainvillea sprouts blossoms. Tonight could produce a bumper crop.

Those three great American fascinations—celebrity, money, and sex—are all flowing freely tonight. Bruce and Demi and Sly and Dustin and the Reverend Jesse are at Caesars tonight, watching Evander Holyfield regain the title belt from a pudgy Riddick Bowe. Guys you've never heard of before are here, too: a supermarket-chain owner from Connecticut; Minnesota's King of Tires; the largest chemical distributor in Oklahoma. When the fight's over, the gamblers will throw so much money at the tables it will make you nauseous. Sure, to them the wagers are just so many colorful chips. But to the amazed onlookers, momentarily distracted from the quarter slots, their gargantuan bets are a new Ford Escort, the oldest child's freshman-year tuition, the down payment on a golf-course condo.

The big boys attend Fight Night primarily to be seen, to mingle with the famous and powerful, to assert their place in the society of High Rollerville. They go because they can.

Stars. Newsmakers. The most prodigious gamblers on the planet—they're all here at Caesars Palace tonight. And so is a man named Ron.

To describe Ron would be difficult, because although he has a distinctive hairstyle, prominent facial features, and a stylish wardrobe, none of these outward trappings really belong to him. This gold-encrusted playboy swaggering through the Fight Night crowd with a deliciously naughty blonde on one hand and a tumbler of whiskey in another appears to be one more ignorant high roller heading toward the $500-minimum blackjack tables, prepared to blow off $30,000 or so in pursuit of a night's diversion.

In fact, this particular high roller is the creation of a $1,000-a-day makeup artist who, through the magic of latex prosthetics and costume jewelry, has transformed Ron from a nerdy nebbish into a flashy cover boy. And not only will Ron not lose the stack of $1,000 chips before him, he might win something approaching $50,000—or as much as he thinks he can get away with. Because although he looks like one of the crowd, an interchangeable extravagantly wealthy man in search of a good time, Ron is at Caesars Palace to work. He is here to count cards.

"You've got to love these Fight Nights," Ron says, surveying the pulsing casino. "They're about the only time guys like me can still make a score."

An expert card counter can obliterate the usual house advantage in blackjack. Where novices take the worst of it and accomplished basic-strategy players get an almost even proposition, the talented counter actually has an edge of a couple percentage points over the casino. While a 1% or 2% advantage may not seem like much, consider this: The house edge at craps or baccarat is even less, yet the gambling emporiums in the desert seem to have little trouble keeping the neon glowing along Las Vegas Boulevard.

Statistically speaking, for every $1,000 the expert counter puts into action, his expected return is around $1,015. Playing three spots at an average of $2,000 a hand, players like Ron have a positive expectation of around $90 for every round of cards they're dealt. A good dealer can easily deal 100 rounds per hour, and perhaps double that to a lone player. So although Ron's edge may initially seem infinitesimal, when supported by a large bankroll and speedy turnover, it is, in fact, enough to make a monster profit. Enough that Ron hasn't had to hold down a "real" job since he was a teenager.

* * *

Learning the basic tenets of card counting is nearly as easy as mastering the rules of blackjack; putting them to practical use is the difficult part. Contrary to a popular misconception, card counters do not, Rainman-like, memorize every card in the deck. They cannot tell you, for example, whether the queen of clubs has been used or if all the red eights remain to be dealt. Using one of a variety of tracking systems, the card counter tabulates the proportion of "good" cards (aces and ten-values) to "bad" cards (2s through 7s). When the deck is rich in good cards, the player has the best of the game. By closely monitoring the remaining cards, a blackjack counter can accurately vary the size of his bets, wagering the minimum when conditions are unprofitable and increasing his volume when they improve. He can also adjust his playing strategy—when to hit, stand, split, double, or surrender—based on the count. Essentially, expert card counters know the right bet and right play at all times.

Understandably, this doesn't thrill the casinos.

Ron's biggest obstacle isn't beating the game, but being allowed to play. One of the most pernicious lies in the gaming industry is the casinos' frequent assertion that they'll welcome anyone's action, win or lose. Despite the undisputed legality of playing blackjack expertly, the truth is casinos throw out card counters faster than you can say "double down." (Casinos are considered private businesses and by law may choose whom they will and won't serve.) Whether you're a $5 or a $100 bettor, if you play the game too well, you'll be asked to leave.

According to one casino executive at a Strip hotel, "No matter what you bet, if you play expertly you're perceived as a threat. We've got plenty of customers who don't play well. We don't need to have our tables filled with counters." To that end, he explains, casinos employ pit bosses trained to recognize expert play, surveillance crews armed with computer software that recognizes betting patterns of a counter, and most remarkable, a private detective agency, Griffin Investigations, which maintains and distributes to its casino clients photos and bios of known counters. For players like Ron, walking into virtually any casino in the world without an elaborate disguise is nearly impossible.

"I've tried to play in some of the new Indian casinos and the riverboats that have opened in the Midwest, but they don't let you bet very much. And when you show any bet variation at all, they get paranoid. They ban you. I've been reduced to playing two or three times a year during very big events, where there's so much money on the table and so much commotion I'm not noticed." He looks at a young man wearing a floor-length fur coat. "These fights are about the only time I get out these days."

His greatest challenge, Ron says, is acting the part. Bookish and soft-spoken away from the casino, Ron labors to appear boisterous and boorish at the tables. "I have genuine difficulty ordering around the floor personnel, yelling for drinks, insulting the dealers. But it's all part of doing business."

* * *

Ron began his peculiar career in the late '70s while attending college at an esteemed university within striking distance of Atlantic City. An economics major with an astounding facility for numbers, he became interested in card counting after reading Ed Thorp's seminal blackjack book, *Beat the Dealer*. Curious but incredulous, Ron and a few friends trekked to the Boardwalk to experiment with what they'd learned. "We started out betting the minimum, getting a feel for the game, growing more confident with the theories," Ron says. "By the time we got our degrees, we'd mastered a couple of multi-level counting systems and increased our bets substantially. I must have won $50,000 in college alone."

Shunning a life in academia, Ron moved to Nevada, where he joined a six-member syndicate that developed a computer that could track various styles of casino shuffling. By inputting data with his toes to a keyboard hidden in his shoe, Ron and his teammates could successfully predict whole clusters of cards based on how the dealer mixed the deck. Because their computer was only marginally based on high-card vs. low-card proportions, Ron's syndicate was seldom suspected of card counting. "Each of us cleared in the high six figures every year," he claims.

In 1986, though, using computers—concealed or not—became illegal in Nevada. After a confederate was severely beaten in the basement of a well-known Strip casino, Ron returned to straight card counting. "It became almost impossible to make a good living," he recalls. "I was banned from just about every casino in the world. Forget Vegas; I couldn't even play in Europe. One week a friend and I tried to play in the Bahamas. They made us give back all our winnings, maybe fifty-thousand dollars, and we each spent a night in jail. The world—not just Vegas—has grown intolerant of counters."

But on Fight Night that all changes. Card counters are like a gang of convicts on a work furlough.

* * *

Perched on the edge of his chair, resting a hand salaciously low on the blonde's back (she's an escort rented for the evening), Ron appears to be concentrating on everything in Caesars but the cards. He's joking with the dealer, splashing his $500 and $1,000 chips in messy piles, casting lascivious glances at the seductively clad women strolling past. You can see what the pit boss is thinking behind his obsequious smile: "What a fool."

For nearly an hour, Ron bets near the minimum, seldom changing the size of his bets despite the occasional richness of the deck. He is, however, letting his companion play a spot every so often, in effect doubling his wager. After a few shoes, Ron and his lady are up a few thousand dollars. A small crowd begins to gather around his table, whispering and nodding at his stack of chips. But Ron doesn't seem to notice. Apparently, he's more interested in working his fingers into his companion's dress.

A crowd, according to Ron, provides good cover. The casino is loath to eject a customer—especially one who's betting so big—in front of other patrons. So after losing his previous three hands, beaten by a flurry of low cards, Ron makes his move.

Looking like a bitter drunk miffed at losing his last three in a row, Ron covers four different spots with $2,000 each. The pit boss takes a step closer to the table. Ron's escort, seemingly of her own volition, takes a handful of chips and stacks them on top of Ron's chips. She looks hopefully at him for approval.

"What the hell!" he blurts. "You feel lucky? Go ahead, go ahead. It's only money!"

The table is loaded with $20,000 in chips. Ron has successfully increased his usual wager nearly 20-fold. And the deck is clearly in his favor.

The dealer has an 8 up. The escort breathlessly announces Ron's totals as the cards hit the layout: 20, blackjack, 12, 19.

Ron hits the 12 and busts. He stands on the others.

The dealer flips over her hole card, a ten. Ron wins three out of four, a $12,500 profit.

The deck is no longer as rich as it was 30 seconds ago. Ron must be tempted to return to something resembling the minimum bet. Instead, to the crowd's delight—and no doubt the pit boss', too—he yells, "Let it ride! What the hell! Double the son of a bitch!"

His escort stacks the chips into $10,000 columns. The pit boss grins nervously. The dealer takes a deep breath. And before a card can be dealt, Ron spills his drink all over the table.

His escort shakes her head. "That, my dear, is bad luck," she says, pulling back his bets. "Even I know that."

"Yeah, I know," Ron says to nobody in particular. Pushing the dealer two $100 chips, Ron gathers his money and stumbles to the next table.

Well into the wee hours of the morning, Ron continues to work. As the sun rises on Las Vegas, when the all-night gamblers start to drink black coffee instead of whiskey, Ron quits. He's up nearly $90,000.

"I gotta stop," he says to the dealer. "I can feel my luck changing." Ron leaves one more tip and smiles at the pit boss.

"You can never be too superstitious," Ron announces. "Especially when it comes to cards."

5

Comp City

"How much does a guy have to lose in this joint before they start taking care of him?" Max Rubin demands, dumping $3,000 worth of black $100 chips onto one of the MGM Grand casino's blackjack tables. It's Fight Night at the MGM this evening, a few-times-a-year occasion for high rollers from around the globe to convene in a glamorous casino, where they can be seen and socialize and gamble and, if they get around to it, observe from a palpably intimate perspective George Foreman getting his face pounded by the German champion.

Dressed in a casually rich track suit, accessorized by a "Shadow Creek" golf hat usually worn only by the loftiest of rollers, Max Rubin would blend in effortlessly with the MGM's spiffy crowd of gamblers, if that was what he wanted.

It's not. "Damn! I've been losing my ass in this joint since lunchtime and I only find out just *now* they're having some sort of fight here tonight," Rubin announces loudly to nobody in particular. A harried pit boss, trying to attend to the needs of several dozen "preferred customers"—that is, wealthy suckers—approaches Rubin's blackjack table. "Something I can do for you, sir?"

"Hell, yeah," Rubin snorts, simultaneously slamming back a "shot" of apple juice and placing a $200 bet. "I've been playing my butt off all day, and this is all I have left," Rubin complains, gesturing toward his pile of chips. Knowing that the shifts have just changed at this pit, Rubin is certain the floorman, who has been on duty only 10 minutes, won't have the time or inclination to check up on his claim. If he did, he would discover Max Rubin had walked into the MGM only five minutes ago.

The pit boss looks Rubin over. You can almost hear his mind working: *"Big player. A little drunk. The kind of loud loser that might alienate my other players. Better keep him happy."* He shakes Rubin's hand. "How can I help you, sir?"

"I hear you got a fight here tonight," Rubin says, as if he were the last guy in the world to notice that 10,000 big shots, celebrities, and Germans happened to have all showed up at the same place this evening.

"That's right, sir. Would you like to see the fight?" the pit boss offers.

"Sure I would," Rubin says. "Could you do that for me?"

"Of course," the pit boss replies. "Just give me your name and I'll call it in to the box office." As he turns to fill out the requisite paperwork, Rubin, who has stopped betting his black chips, calls the pit boss back.

"Hey, could you make that for two?" The pit boss hesitates for a millisecond.

"Sure I can."

"'Preciate that, pardner." As the pit boss shuffles off, Rubin, dropping the Texas drawl and drunken slur, turns to me and smiles. "Got 'em!" he says, picking up his chips. "Is this a great town or what?"

With $900 worth of prime-location fight tickets in hand, we amble to the MGM Grand Garden arena where, along with Jim Carrey, Magic Johnson, Arsenio and Montel, and thousands of other glittering VIPs, we'll see George Foreman slink away with one of the most undeserved victories in recent heavyweight history. And thanks to Max Rubin's knowledge of the casino business, it won't cost us more than a few dollars.

Nor do the limos, the suites, the gourmet meals, the

show tickets, the booze, or the afternoon of golf. It's all comped.

Max Rubin is the author of *Comp City: A Guide to Free Las Vegas Vacations*, the first book to reveal the inner workings of the Las Vegas comp system, a widely known but little understood marketing tool the casinos use to lure premium players to their tables. Formerly a casino executive, Rubin saw first-hand how Las Vegas casinos doled out more than half a billion dollars in comps per year, solely to encourage their customers to gamble (and lose) more. "The gambling business is a cat-and-mouse game," Rubin says, as we cruise down the Strip in our complimentary limousine. "Guess who's the mouse?"

Comp City is helping to change the game into one of cat and dog—and the hounds are beginning to chase the kitties up a tree. "The book contains information the general public was never supposed to find out," Rubin remarks. "These are the casino industry's most guarded secrets."

According to the author, the casino complimentary system is designed to give back to the player approximately 40¢ for every $1 in gambling losses. His book shows how to exploit numerous loopholes in the comp system to earn $1 back for every 10¢-30¢ in losses.

Casino expert Steve Forte says *Comp City* is the most important gambling book to be published in the last 10 years. "I've always thought the subject of comps would make a great book, and nobody knows more about them than Max. Anybody who regularly gives casinos their action should read this book first."

Heeding Forte's advice, I devoured the 291-page book in two sittings and was surprised at how generous—and how vulnerable—the casinos can be with their freebies. Using a technique Rubin dubs ACES (Advanced Comp Equivalency Strategy), clever comp hustlers—those who can play a solid game of blackjack, convincingly represent their ability to lose a lot of money, and have no fear of asking for unearned rewards—can enjoy the fabulous perks most people believe are reserved exclusively for the super rich.

Still, even after digesting Rubin's entertaining and re-velatory investigation, which reads like a comical how-to primer in larceny, I was skeptical. Though the mathemati-cal explanations in *Comp City* couldn't be clearer and Rubin's writing has the ring of true authority, I wondered if the book's techniques would work in the real world, with a pit boss breathing over my shoulder. "The only way the tech-niques in this book don't work is if you have moral and ethical qualms about taking thousands of dollars in good-ies from the casinos," Rubin claimed. "Course, the casinos don't have any problem bankrupting you."

I decided to see for myself.

Following the advice in *Comp City*, I called six Vegas hotels to ascertain which was most eager for my business. Posing as a black-chip player anxious to gamble it up on the big fight weekend, I was connected with executive hosts, whose job is to attract well-financed suckers to the tables—then keep them there. I told them they could expect $100-a-hand-and-up action from me. What, I politely inquired, could I expect in return? As Rubin's book predicted, the fancier joints were not particularly impressed. The Mirage told me they couldn't promise me anything until they saw my action. The Treasure Island said I could expect to be comped into a mini-suite, but shouldn't count on meals above and beyond the coffee shop. Luxor said my action would warrant a jacuzzi suite and *maybe* food and bever-age, depending on my play. The Golden Nugget promised me full RFB (room, food, and beverage) for $150-per-hand action at four hours of play a day, but said for a suite I'd have to show them $200-$250 per hand. Still, with no de-posit, no up-front money in the cage, nothing more than my name and a telephone number—and a faint promise of action—each property gave me a guaranteed reservation on nights that had been "sold out" for weeks.

The less of a name brand, the more willing the casinos were to treat me like royalty. At the Frontier, a mid-Strip hotel (which, at the time, had been plagued by striking cu-linary union workers for over a year), I was put through directly to one of the shift managers, who said that black-chip action would entitle me to full RFB, including accommodations in one of the atrium tower suites. "If you give us that kind of play, you can have the run of the place," the boss told me.

Meanwhile, the Lady Luck, downtown, had been making an aggressive pitch at uptown players, taking out full-page advertisements in many of the in-flight magazines. The ads promised "green chip" ($25) players all the spoils of the big-name joints: gourmet dining, spacious suites, fully stocked limos—the works. What, I wondered, would the Lady Luck do for a black-chip player?

"Anything you want," a host told me. I could almost hear him drooling on the other end of the telephone. Completely unbidden, he offered me full RFB, show tickets, *and* golf. "Anywhere you want to play!" For four hours a day of $50 bets, all this could be mine. For double the action, I might have a shot at the ultimate comp: tickets to the heavy-weight title fight.

Using conversion tables contained in *Comp City*, I quickly calculated the expected cost of my high-roller weekend: approximately $40. I knew I could play the Lady Luck's single-deck blackjack game at about a .2% disadvantage. At $50 a hand, I could expect to lose around $5 an hour. Eight hours of required play would cost me less than the price of taking my girlfriend to dinner and the movies.

So why would the Lady Luck—or any casino, for that matter—be so eager to wine and dine such a meager producer? Because, as Rubin's book explains, they think you're losing more than you really are. The casino figures the average player to give up a 2% disadvantage at 21, but part of being what Rubin calls a "comp wizard" is learning how to play perfect basic strategy blackjack. (It takes about 30 minutes to learn and is explained clearly in the book.) The casino figures 75-100 hands per hour rate of play, but the comp wizard effectively slows the game down to 50 hands or less, reducing the casino's total handle dramatically. The casino is prepared to give back almost half the player's expected losses in comps, but the comp wizard knows how to squeeze out a 1,000% return.

Upon arrival at the Lady Luck, the afternoon before the big Foreman fight, I met Max Rubin at the casino's cage where, under the watchful eye of an executive host, I deposited a bankroll of $10,000, most of which I had no intention of touching. The host immediately made dinner reservations for us that evening in the hotel's gourmet restaurant, the Burgundy Room.

After a brief meeting in my deluxe accommodations, where we sipped complimentary champagne and discussed playing strategy and tableside demeanor (pleasant but needy), we made our first play. Finding a table with several other patrons and a slow dealer, we settled into two empty seats, flashed a fistful of hundreds, and ordered whiskeys and cigars. A pit boss immediately gravitated to our table and made a formal introduction. With her hovering at my side, I made a few $200 bets, making sure my oversized action was duly noted. When she went to attend to other business, I scaled my wagers back to $50 and $75. An hour later—following a leisurely 10-minute break to "make a telephone call"—three men in suits approached me with their arms outstretched. One was the Director of this and another was the Director of that, and they all wanted to tell me how pleased they were to have me as their honored guest, and, oh, by the way, anything I possibly might need, please, let them know.

One of them reserved the best seats in the house for the Lady Luck's magic show; the other handed me a gold plastic card that entitled me to complimentary meals in any of their restaurants, complimentary room service, and limousine transportation wherever I pleased.

"Not bad," Rubin said, laughing, "for an hour's worth of play. Give them a few more hours and we can ask for golf and seats at the fight."

After three hours of play, strategically interrupted by two more 10-minute breaks and a few major stalls while I chatted with my new executive pals, I pushed in my chips and asked the pit boss how I was doing on my rating (the casino's method of quantifying a player's level of action). "You're a solid two-hundred-dollar-a-hand player. Everything will be taken care of," I was told.

"I guess he didn't notice your twenty-five-dollar bets," Rubin said later, smiling. "What was your real average? Around seventy-five dollars?" He suggested I inquire about fight tickets at this point, before the casino figured out that $1,100 of the $1,200 I had "lost" ended up in the pockets of my suit.

A fruit and cheese basket was waiting in my room upon my return. So was a liter bottle of Stolichnaya. The booze and our upcoming meal, I calculated, was already worth more than the $100 I had dropped. But what if I'd lost more, I asked Rubin. Is it worth losing thousands of dollars in the pursuit of comps?

He explained that most people who come to Vegas lose their money anyway, but don't get any of the perquisites to which they're entitled. The comp wizard, on the other hand, knows precisely the expected loss of his play and the expected gain of his comps, and usually the schism between the two is not even close. [See Box.] But expected loss does not always translate to actual loss: Blackjack is volatile; deviations happen. I could easily have lost several thousand in my first three hours. But I also could have won several thousand—fluctuations go both ways. In fact, Rubin reminded me, he and the tournament blackjack expert, Anthony Curtis, won $2,200 in 45 minutes going after four $200 tickets to the Rolling Stones' Voodoo Lounge concert—*and* they nabbed the tickets. "Our expected loss in the 'Voodoo' play was forty-five dollars," Rubin explained. "We ended up with a three-thousand-dollar profit."

At the nadir of my comped weekend, I was down nearly $3,800. At the zenith I was up $2,400. (Playing with black chips, the swings are quick.) At the end of my play, after several gluttonous meals, a round of golf at the Desert Inn Country Club, and—of course—the ultimate prize, the fight ticket, I was a $24 winner. Heeding Rubin's advice from

Comp City, I plowed my profits into a commemorative Foreman vs. Schulz T-shirt, a $22 investment that I could give to my executive host as a token of my appreciation for taking such good care of me. "That will pay big dividends," Rubin predicted.

He was right. Next time I want to visit the Lady Luck, the host informed me, the airfare's on him.

BANG FOR THE BUCK
A Comp Accounting

THE HOUSE EDGE

Total Playing Time ...... 6.5 Hours

Average Bet $75

House Edge .... .19%

Expected Loss .... [$46]

THE PLAYER'S GAIN

Two Nights' Room $600

Meals $425

Limos $100

Show Tickets $60

Liquor $50

Golf $165

Fight Ticket......................... $300

Return Airfare $144

Total Comp Value $1,844

Less Cost .... –$46

NET GAIN **$1,798**

6

Out of the Oscars,
Into the Pan

If you were to pick a single night of the year when you might reasonably expect the streets of Los Angeles to be bereft of traffic, a night when the stores would be empty and the living rooms full, the fourth Monday in March would be an excellent candidate. This particular night, you may recall, is Oscar Night, that annual spectacle of glamorous, self-congratulatory Hollywood excess, when most of the world—especially the residents of Los Angeles—drop what they're doing and park in front of a television.

Pan players, however, are not most of the world.

While the members of the Academy of Motion Picture Arts and Sciences are handing out their statuettes, hardcore pan addicts are safely ensconced at the Commerce Casino, near downtown Los Angeles, playing their favorite game, oblivious to the vagaries of Best Adapted Screenplay and Outstanding Lifetime Achievement in sound editing. Their attention is focused on what it's always focused on: a big eight-deck block of playing cards with all the 8s, 9s, and 10s removed. Occasionally one of the panners looks up at a big-screen television hovering over the little, round, seven-player table long enough to note, "Oh, what's his name won Best Actor... Is it my turn?" But aside from these momentary distractions, this night is very much like any other night. Oscars-Shmoscars.

I don't mean to suggest that pan players are any more degenerate than their poker-playing brethren, many hundreds of whom are also out in full force on Oscar Night. But because the game they play is shrouded in mystery—no one under the age of 40, it seems, knows how pan is played—the pan pit has the foreboding aura of a secret society. It's the opium den of the casino. You get the sense that pan's pull, its addictive quality, is so compelling that not only would the Commerce regulars blithely forego the Academy Awards broadcast, they would likely prefer a rousing game of pan to watching the first televised images of a man walking on Jupiter. Or Bill Clinton with his clothes off.

I decided to see what all the fuss was about.

My only knowledge of the game, gleaned from passing pan tables on the way to poker games, was that the players often used the eraser end of pencils to pluck cards from an oversized stack. And that you played not for points or pots or limits but for "konditions," an oblique neologism that seemed to me vaguely sinister and silly. (Did this game have some tenuous association with the Klan? Or Kwickie Marts?) Also, based on casual observation, it appeared to me that to really enjoy this peculiar game, you had to be well on your way to receiving Social Security benefits.

When I called a Commerce pan host to ask how much I might possibly have to invest to get the full flavor of an action-packed pan game, she strongly dissuaded me from playing. "This is not a game you can just sit down and hop right in. You'll lose all your money. And if you don't know all the rules, the players will crucify you."

Ah, just like poker, I thought.

Undeterred—either because I believed my superior intelligence and good looks would see me through pan's supposed minefields, or possibly because I'm a stubborn fool—I decided to join the pan battles without the benefit of a single lesson. My plan was this: I would watch from a comfortable distance, learn the game's rudiments, find an open seat, and crush my unsuspecting opponents—*and* watch snippets of the Oscars out of the corner of my eye. Of course, it might have helped had I known pan's rules (the official notebook the Commerce hands out to its floormen covers 58 different issues). Reading this rule book, drowning in minutiae, I wondered if what little capacity I have left for memory in my increasingly crowded brain wouldn't be better used reading about, say, the Pelopennesian War. Analytical skill, strategy, courage, foresight—forget about it. The most important element in being an accomplished pan player, from what I could gather, was knowing the rules.

This was what I was able to glean: Pan (a shortening of "panguingue," which, in Creole, means "utterly inscrutable game designed to keep elderly gamblers off the streets") is dealt and played counter-clockwise, primarily, I suspect, to further confuse and confound life-long poker players. You start with 10 cards in your hand and are trying to get rid of them all by making melds of three or more cards: "ropes," or straight flushes; and "squares," three or more of the same rank. Most melds allow you simply to reduce your card count; other melds have value and are known as—ah ha!—"konditions." When melding a kondition, you may collect from the other players who have played their hands. (Very key strategy: *Never play your hand unless you've been dealt a lot of valuable konditions.* Once I finally sat down to play, it took me only about two hours of constant donations to figure this out.) Like poker, you may fold your hand after the deal and forfeit your "tops" (ante) bet. In retrospect, this should have been my—and every beginner's—primary strategy, but, like most rookies, I *pan*-icked and played way too many hands. And got slaughtered by a gang of nice old ladies.

The key cards in pan are 3s, 5s, and 7s, especially those in spades. These are the "valle" cards (pronounced "val-ley," as in San Fernando, or more appropriately given my introduction to pan, Death), which help you earn the bulk of your konditions.

Pan has another quirky rule: When you set down a

kondition, you must *ask* to be paid by the other players. (Imagine such a convention at your regular stud game.) On Oscar Night, the tone of such requests ranged from congenial ("Two, please?") to combative ("That'll be three more!") to, in my case, profoundly confused ("Do I get any chips now?").

Pan has an evocative glossary that, if you didn't know better, you might think was authored by a gang of horny truck drivers stoned on Maui Wowee. When someone goes out before you do, you've been "peckered." A hand of no value is a "pisser." When you get rid of your cards nearly all at once, you "undress" yourself. And 3-of-a-kind in spades is known as a "bong."

The dealer is not called a dealer. He's a "mucker."

But of all the customs you must know about pan, this is the most important: When you pluck a card, lay it on the table—*do not ever put a card into your hand.* Thanks to years of gin rummy conditioning, I almost committed this mortal sin about nine times and was threatened with decapitation or worse on each occasion. "You do that again, I'll hit ya'," one nice lady promised me.

To say panners are, as a group, remarkably rude, mean-spirited, and bitter would be a gross exaggeration. Only about half of them are. The other half appear to be very happy. Pan gives them ample opportunity to socialize, gamble, and, under the camouflage of "discarding," throw cards at dealers.

To my uninitiated eyes on Oscar Night, the game moved blindingly fast, with the players more or less running the show. (Dealers actually switch tables in the middle of hands.) To a first-time panner, the game seems to be somewhat similar to gin rummy, only about 20 times as complicated. Even after several hours of play, I could not discern what distinguished a good panner from a bad one, save for having the innate ability to be dealt good cards. Indeed, one kindly old man, noting my confusion, said, "Believe it or not, there is a degree of strategy in this game. Probability and such."

"How much skill?" I asked.

"Oh, about five percent. All the rest is luck."

Indeed, one floorman confided to me that pan was basically a game of chance, with a slight premium placed on how you maneuver your cards through the melding process. Most of your success or failure is a result of gauging which "starting hands" are worth playing.

Easy.

The floorman found me a seat in the smallest game, a $1 kondition. I bought in for $20. The other players immediately pegged me for a rank novice, probably because I had an open rule book placed next to my chips.

"I never read a rule book in my life, and I've been playing forty years," one lady named Margie volunteered. "How long you been playing?"

"About thirty seconds," I told her.

"No!"

"Yes."

"Most people learn in home games. You're gonna try to learn here?"

I told her I was. On my inaugural pan hand I lost $7. On the next one I lost $4. "I'm improving!" I said hopefully.

"Honey," Margie said, "can I give you some advice? You're not ready to play for money. Just watch a little; try to learn from what I'm doing. Watch close now—or I'll hit ya'!"

I snuck a peek at the Oscars telecast. "You want to learn a little or not?!"

For the next hour Margie became my unofficial pan tutor, showing me which hands to play, which to discard; when to pluck, when to discard; when to ask for payment, when to shut up. She was patient and kind and instructive, very much like my grandmother—except for when she threatened to slap me for putting a card in my hand. With Margie's help I managed to win two or three hands. And lose about 17 others.

In three hours I somehow ran through $100, two or three depressing dollars at a time. (What can I say? Most of my hands were pissers, and so frequently was I peckered I never managed to go out on a bong even once!) Despite my slowness, my occasional breaches of pan etiquette, my moronic questions, I suspect the other players were exceedingly happy to have me at their table.

"Come back soon," they said as I got up to leave, having failed to "go out" on a single hand. "You know where to find us!"

Indeed, I do. Whether it's Oscar Night or Super Sunday or Election Eve, my pan pals will still be there, plucking and discarding and politely asking to be paid. But here's the sad part: I fear I might be there, too.

7

The $17 Million Man

Las Vegas is a city built on myths. Lies, really. They range from the innocuous ("Certain slot machines are 'ready' to pay off") to the inane ("You can beat keno with the right system"). None of the Vegas myths is bigger, though, than the one that goes like this: "It's possible to drift into town with only a few bucks and leave a week later with a fortune." That's the elemental Vegas myth, the one that turns normally responsible men into fools and pensioners into paupers. Were it not for the gambling public's unwavering faith in the Big Myth, Las Vegas' casinos wouldn't win billions a year. Hotel rooms wouldn't cost $39. And shrimp cocktails couldn't be had for 99 cents.

With every quarter dropped down a slot machine, every dollar bet on blackjack, every parlay card wagered at the sports book, gamblers harbor an inchoate fantastic hope that their meager plunge might lead to something big. They dream they might be the lucky soul who makes the Vegas myth come true.

The fact is, it never happens.

Sure, countless suckers have built a piddling bankroll into several thousand dollars, and, yes, the statewide Megabucks progressive slot jackpot gets hit every so often, making someone an instant millionaire—over a 20-year payout period. Statistical deviations do happen.

But no one, no one, has ever churned mere bus fare into truly big money. Mansion-in-Bel-Air and yacht-in-the-Caribbean money. Mythic money.

No one, that is, until Archie Karas.

If not for the John Gotti hairstyle and two demure gold-and-diamond pinkie rings, you might think he was some sort of businessman, an executive at a respectable corporation, not an inveterate gambler. Archie Karas dresses stylishly but unprepossessingly, foregoing the loud track suits and ostentatious gold-nugget bracelets many of his colleagues favor. (He's got $20,000 watches, but most days he wears a Seiko.) His clean-cut grooming is impeccable, far from the haggard visage of someone who spends entirely too much time in the stale environs of a casino. His nails are always clean.

But his domain is not the boardroom. It's the cardroom.

Some consider him a hopeless degenerate. Some think he's a hero. Others think he's insane.

Archie Karas, 43, likes to be referred to as the Undisputed Champion of Gambling. "I've gambled more money than anyone in the history of the planet," he claims. "What most gamblers make in their whole life, I gamble in one roll of the dice. Unless the casinos decide to raise their limits after I'm gone, I don't think anyone will ever gamble more than I have. I'm the biggest ever."

Prior to 1992 Archie was similar to hundreds of other gamblers: He'd win; he'd lose; one day he'd be driving a Mercedes-Benz, the next he'd be sleeping in it. When he went broke, he'd borrow a grubstake and start over. The usual. His career, if you can call it that, has been a series of phenomenal successes and abject failures—and not much in between. "I've been a millionaire over fifty times and dead broke more than I can count. Probably a thousand times in my life," Archie recalls. "But I sleep the same whether I have ten or ten million dollars in my pocket."

After immigrating to America from Greece at 17—working on a freighter for $60 a month, he jumped ship in Portland, Oregon—Archie got a job as a waiter in a Los Angeles restaurant. The restaurant was next door to a bowling alley. In that bowling alley were several pool tables. Around those pool tables were dozens of marks ready to be fleeced. A hustler was born.

Still a teenager, new to the Land of Opportunity, Archie learned to play pool and poker, eventually cleaning out the restaurant's owner. He had the kind of epiphany then that comes to most people upon retirement from a lifetime of labor, or after hitting the lottery: "I knew at eighteen that I'd never have to work." He also thought if he ever won $10,000 he'd be set forever. That figure was revised upward to $100,000, then $500,000, then $1 million. Now he knows he'll never stop.

In December 1992 Archie lost nearly $2 million in high-stakes card games at the legal Los Angeles-area casinos. For the thousandth-and-first time in his life, he was broke.

He drove into Las Vegas with $50.

Unlike the Social Security matron with a couple of twenties in her stockings or the drunk with a roll of quarters stuffed in his pocket, Archie knew his dearth of capital wouldn't prevent him from making a score. No hole was too big for him to climb out of.

He headed to the Mirage, where a fellow gambler lent him $10,000 to take a shot at the biggest action in the cardroom, a $200-$400 razz game. (Razz is seven-card stud played for low, the best hand being A-2-3-4-5.) He promptly won $20,000. After returning half the profits to his backer, who was thrilled to realize a 100% gain in only a few hours, Archie had the seeds of a bankroll that would eventually lead to what Vegas cognoscenti now refer to simply as "the Run."

Archie bristles at the suggestion that his streak was anything more than just another series of gambles in a lifetime of wagering, that he momentarily got luckier than anyone else has ever gotten. Even as a kid, he'll tell you, he always bet everything he had, and he always played the best, only champions. The Run, he insists, was no different. Only bigger.

It started, as many of Archie's adventures have, at a pool table. There, playing against a high-ranking executive of a well-known hotel corporation for stakes that reliable sources say were $10,000 a game and up, Archie won between $1 million and $2 million. For the sake of his opponent's reputation, Archie refuses to discuss details of the match, saying only, "The pool was no big deal. I played against a lot of people, and I'm not going to confirm or deny any amounts that have been talked about." Despite his diplomacy, the "facts" of Archie's pool match were reported in the *Las Vegas Review-Journal,* and are widely known among the gambling community, as is the loser's identity.

This man, call him Mr. B., is a world-class poker player, whose victories over the toughest competition on the planet have been well-documented. Realizing pool was clearly Archie's kingdom, Mr. B. suggested moving the battle to another green-felt arena, the poker table, where Mr. B. thought he was the odds-on favorite. In early 1993, after a week of heads-up play, Archie beat him out of another million.

The reason you or I will never win several million dollars gambling is because we are rational reasonable people. We'd never get to the lofty point where millions of dollars are on the line, because we would quit as soon as we won $50,000 or $20,000 or even $10,000.

Archie Karas doesn't know the word quit.

After crushing Mr. B., Archie welcomed all comers, defying anyone to beat him at a one-on-one poker match. In April 1993 during the World Series of Poker at Binion's Horseshoe, his first challenger was David "Chip" Reese, one of the few living members of the Poker Hall of Fame and generally considered the best all-around poker player in the world.

Reese is a fat man with thinning blond hair, an omnipresent cellular phone, and a poker pedigree rivaled by few others, living or dead. He and his equally accomplished pal, two-time World Champ Doyle Brunson, consistently play in the largest games in town and have probably beaten more contenders and pretenders out of the richest pots in Vegas than anyone who's ever held a full house. Multi-millionaire businessmen, knowing they have little chance of winning, often play with the duo just to say they lost to the best.

In the middle of the Horseshoe's tournament room, where $25-$50 and $50-$100 games are common, Archie, with his newly minted bankroll, and Chip, competing with the financial backing of a famous hotel owner, played razz and seven-card stud for unthinkable stakes: $3,000-$6,000, $4,000-$8,000, and eventually, according to Archie, $8,000-$16,000 limits. In approximately two weeks, Archie beat the putative champ for $2,022,000.

Resigning from the game, Reese supposedly told Archie, "God made your balls a little bigger. You're too good."

Rather than plowing his winnings into long-term certificates of deposit or even, heaven forbid, a savings account, Archie started "investing" his winnings at the Horseshoe's crap tables. Throughout late spring and early summer '93, he rolled the dice regularly, betting $100,000 and more on every toss of the cubes. "With each play I was making million-dollar decisions," Archie says. "I would have played even higher if they'd let me."

The irony in all this was that Archie Karas was known to the casino as a notorious cheat. This is not something he likes to talk about. But his name, picture, and "rap sheet" of suspected maneuvers fill nearly a full page in the Griffin Book, an encyclopedic security resource for casinos compiled by a private detective agency. For years he had allegedly been a dice slider and a card marker, and generally violated whatever rules of fair play he could do without. And for years he got by. Now, playing on the square, with every surveillance camera in the joint focused on his action, Archie Karas was winning exponentially more than he ever had as a rule-breaker.

At his request, the Horseshoe closed down a table for him, providing a solitary battleground for Archie and his compulsion. As armed security guards surrounded the table and dozens of awestruck onlookers craned for a peek at the numbered layout laden with chips, Archie rolled to winning sessions of $1.6 million, $900,000, $800,000, $1.3 million, and $4 million. At one point he had all of Binion's chocolate-colored $5,000 chips.

He also claims to have booked losers of $2 million, $2.5 million, $2.3 million, and $1.5 million.

Exactly how much Archie Karas won (or lost) playing craps is difficult to verify, and in some ways, irrelevant. No matter the final tally, this much is clear: Archie was rolling for millions, while six months earlier the man had $50 to his name.

The craps, Archie tells me, was merely a diversion when the poker action dried up. "I know I'm taking the worst of it with the dice," Archie says. "But nobody would play poker with me for that much."

Indeed, after Reese was vanquished, few players had either the gumption or the bankroll to tangle with the man who was now calling himself the uncrowned World Champion. One who did was Stu Ungar, a three-time World Series of Poker victor, known for his hyper-aggressive raise-it-to-the-roof style. Yards away from where his picture hangs in Binion's Gallery of Champions, playing $5,000-$10,000 limit stud and razz with a backer's money, Ungar took just six hours to lose $900,000.

Next, the legendary Brunson took his shot at breaking Archie. The best he could do was break even. "We stopped after a while," Archie reports. "He didn't want to play high enough."

In quick succession, Hall of Famers and World Champions came and went, including Mr. B. again, Puggy Pearson, and Johnny Chan. Of the poker community's elite, only Chan ever beat Archie—after losing to him three straight times.

At the Run's end, Archie had busted 15 of the world's greatest, winning $7 million at the poker table.

"Playing poker at this level is like boxing," Archie says. "You have to keep defending your title. Except a boxer gets six months to recover between fights. I take them on one after another. And I only play champions." He shrugs. "Nobody wants to play me anymore."

Jim Albrecht, the poker manager at the Horseshoe, witnessed some of Archie's epic run. He thinks that part of the reason none of the top poker players will compete against Archie is because of the stakes. "Even if you think you have an edge, playing cards at five-thousand or ten-thousand-dollar limits is like Russian Roulette," Albrecht observes. "If I use a gun with two bullets and give you one with one bullet, you're a big favorite to live longer than me. But are you going to play? It's suicidal."

Archie Karas, according to Albrecht, reminds him of another famous gambler with the same heritage, Nick "The Greek" Dandolos. "Nick's credo was always, 'Find me the biggest and best and we'll play until someone's broke.'"

Archie has a standing offer: He'll play anyone for any amount, preferably for $500,000 or more. I ask him if he'd be willing to compete for every penny he has—if, for instance, the Sultan of Brunei wanted to play a friendly freeze-out for, say, $15 million.

"In a second," Archie replies.

"You've got to understand something. Money means nothing to me. I don't value it," Archie explains. "I've had all the material things I could ever want. Everything. The things I want money can't buy: health, freedom, love, happiness. I don't care about money, so I have no fear. I don't care if I lose it."

Two months from now Archie Karas may be broke. He may be sleeping in his car, scrounging for a buy-in to a high-stakes poker game. He may be just another lonely soul staring at the boulevard's flashing lights, dreaming of parlaying his last handful of change into a mountain of cash.

But he'll always know that for several glorious odds-defying months, he made the Vegas myth come true.

At the Racetrack

8

The Andy-capper

Everyone who knows anything about gambling knows this: You can't win betting the horses. Too big of a house take-out, too much "vig." No matter how sharp your handicapping, no matter how fool-proof your system, the oppressive mathematics of the game (about a 20% disadvantage) eventually grind up even the wisest guy. Damon Runyon, who wagered on a pony or two in his time, put it this way: "All horse players die broke."

Almost all.

Andrew Beyer is not broke. Andrew Beyer is not well on his way to dying penniless and bitter, raving about the sure-thing nag that quit in the backstretch. Andrew Beyer, in fact, is quite sane and happy and financially solvent.

Which, as horse players go, is saying something. Then again, Andrew Beyer is considered by many in the business to be the best—and most important—handicapper in America.

Michael "Roxy" Roxborough, the man who sets the Vegas line and an avid horse player, says of Beyer, "When Andrew Beyer walks through the grandstand of any racetrack in America, he's the most recognizable person in the crowd. He has more enthusiasm for betting on horses than anyone in the sport."

If you don't know who Andrew Beyer is, you probably

don't bet on horses. If you do, you're probably aware that Beyer, 54, the author of four best-selling books on handicapping, is the syndicated horse racing columnist for the *Washington Post,* a position he's held since 1978. To those who regularly peruse the *Daily Racing Form,* the horse-bettor's bible, his name is legendary: He is the eponymous creator of the revolutionary Beyer Speed Figures, possibly the most powerful tool in horse handicapping since the invention of the stopwatch.

Not long ago, I spent a day at the track with Beyer, getting an insider's view of how he computes his Figures, how he picks the ponies, and, ultimately, how he beats one of the toughest games in the world. In the course of analyzing, betting, and yes, agonizing over a full card of races, Andrew Beyer revealed why he is one of the most interesting characters in the world of gambling.

* * *

When you arrive at Andy Beyer's house, in a woodsy embassy-speckled neighborhood in northwest Washington, D.C., you become immediately aware that it is not the home of a punter struggling to come up with enough spare change to bet the Daily Double. Beyer and his wife, Susan, an interior decorator, live in an airy, modern residence—"one of the twenty houses in Washington that isn't a Colonial," Susan Beyer jokes. Filled with tasteful furniture and beautiful art, there's only one painting in the whole joint that has anything vaguely to do with horse racing, a post-impressionist blur of color and motion depicting a group of ponies charging for the wire.

Andy Beyer's home office is similarly devoid of tacky equine posters, Leroy Neiman action paintings, or portraits of Triple Crown winners on black velvet. Bookshelves filled with hundreds of old *Racing Forms* and a small library of handicapping tomes sit opposite a large desk containing all manner of computers and other electrical accoutrements. The only memento adorning Beyer's otherwise sparse workplace is a framed silver horseshoe, worn by the legendary Secretariat when he won the Bay Shore Stakes at Aqueduct in 1973.

"I'm a numbers guy, not a real visual type," Beyer says. "I have no skill at all judging the physical animal. I can't tell if a horse is feeling badly or if he's ready to run the best race of his life, just by looking at him. My focus is on the fundamentals."

It is this disregard for all that is extraneous and irrelevant—Beyer, in fact, seldom even refers to a horse by its name, only its racing number—that has made him a handicapping success.

Ever since he was 12, when his parents took him to a now-defunct track called Randall Park outside of Cleveland, Andy Beyer has been captivated by handicapping horses. But not because he was intoxicated by the romance or beauty of the sport. His love was born, he explains, of the "puzzle aspect" of picking winners.

"I've always enjoyed games and puzzles. I went through a chess phase and a bridge phase and a long poker phase. I always liked games that had a mathematical component," Beyer tells me, settling into the press box at Baltimore's Pimlico, home of the Preakness. "But I never had world-class ability at any of them. Still, at a very young age the gambling bug was germinating. Pinball, cards, whatever— I liked playing games. As soon as I had my first look at the *Daily Racing Form,* I was entranced."

In high school, Beyer dabbled with an indulgent bookie who took his $1 and $2 bets. When he went on to Harvard, where he was supposed to be majoring in English literature, Beyer spent most of his class-time playing the ponies at Suffolk Downs, getting an advanced degree in going broke. Instead of reading Homer and Shakespeare, he immersed himself in Herbert O. Yardley's classic, *Education of a Poker Player,* and financed his horse racing habit with all-night card games. "I was flying blind," Beyer recalls, making handicapping notes with a red magic marker. "There was little published literature on betting horses at the time.

I decided that if I ever learned enough about horse racing, I would try to become the Yardley of horses."

Beyer never did graduate. His final exam on Chaucer fell on the same date as the Belmont Stakes.

After a string of sportswriter jobs, which barely subsidized his losses at the track, Beyer realized that the two things he wanted to do most were write about racing and learn to win. In 1970, both his dreams started to come true when an editor at the *Washington Daily News* let him write a weekly horse column—and he began experimenting with speed figures.

Previously, like so many desperate horse players, Beyer had stumbled down any number of blind alleys: a system that graded horses on their winning percentage versus number of times in the money; a system that charted the "Z" pattern in a horse's running line; a system that assigned power points based on a horse's pedigree. "All my handicapping was based on angles, not fundamentals. None of these angles ever addressed the key issue: Who is better than whom? The orthodoxy back then said that 'class' was the measure of a race," Beyer explains, making hieroglyphic notations in the margins of his race program. "For instance, if a ten-thousand dollar claimer was running against a slower twenty-thousand dollar claimer, the assumption was that the slower but 'classier' horse would win. I was looking for a way to verify—or contradict—that assumption."

The concept of speed figures by no means originated with Andrew Beyer. A number of now-forgotten handicappers fooled around with them in the 1950s. But no one had ever produced a reliable model that could be trusted over the long run, one that could tell you, for example, if one horse runs six furlongs in 1:11 and another runs seven furlongs in 1:24, which is a better time?

Andrew Beyer took a stack of old *DRF*s and did the laborious math by hand, sifting through years of data, applying the analytical skills he'd developed as a game-playing child. "Six furlongs in one-thirteen equals seven furlongs in one-twenty-six and a fifth was my E equals mc squared," Beyer says, laughing. By 1972 he'd managed to construct a reliable speed chart that incorporated the important element of track variance (a measure of track speed and bias), which was previously calculated by an antiquated—and, in most cases, inaccurate—system. Beyer devised a highly specific sophisticated method for determining track variances, a method that accounted for the times turned in by different types of horses.

By combining his newly minted speed ratings with his fresh perspective on track bias, the young columnist invented the Beyer Speed Figures.

"As crude as they were, the Speed Figures were a revelation," Beyer remembers, gazing happily at the track below, watching the horses load into the starting gate for the first race. "Newton couldn't have been more excited. You've got to understand, class was still the big deal. For example, a horse would win a ten-thousand-dollar claiming race and move up to twenty-thousand dollars and nobody would touch him. And according to my Figures, sometimes this long shot was actually the fastest horse in the field. There were times when I'd be one of three guys out of a thousand that knew this. It was like having the Rosetta Stone."

In those giddy days, Andrew Beyer not only made a handsome profit, but more important to the inveterate horse player, he *understood.* "I'd hit on the core truth of the game. I had a way to measure every horse! Now, the rational decision would have been to forget my job, keep quiet about my discovery, and bet as much as possible," Beyer admits. "But I wanted to be Yardley."

In 1975 Beyer wrote a book outlining the theory and practice behind his Speed Figures. "With a system so complex, I didn't think anyone would be particularly interested." His book, *Picking Winners,* received a rave review from a closet horse player at the *New York Times. Sports Illustrated* wrote that "a generation of Beyer disciples was born." And suddenly, Beyer had what quickly became the best-selling horse book of all time.

Beyer sees an interesting value in the second race at

Pimlico and bets the three horse (Fuelonthefire) in a boxed exacta with the six horse. "The three is a legit four-to-one going off at nine-to-one," Beyer says. "And the six is the second-best horse in this race." Per his prediction, the three runs a valiant race, finishing second to the favorite. The six, though, is never in contention. Beyer nods thoughtfully and continues his story.

Before 1987, when Beyer started selling his Speed Figures to the public, and especially before 1992, when the *DRF* started publishing them, Beyer cashed tickets on plenty of 20- and 30-1 shots. "Them were the days, as they say," Beyer jokes. "But I've never been an entrepreneur. I liked being a writer and a gambler." As the years passed and the Beyer Speed Figures became a widely accepted concept, their creator no longer felt like "the one guy at the track with a magic code."

Indeed, these days the Beyer Speed Figures have become an omnipresent factor in the horse game, so popular that, according to Roxy Roxborough, "The Figures are used not only by handicappers, but by trainers and owners as well. They've become a standard part of the industry."

Beyer himself admits that using his Figures alone is no longer an adequate method for beating horse racing. The formerly proprietary information is now built into the odds, lowering the "price" and often resulting in certain horses being overbet and overvalued. Ponies that might have once gone off at 25-1 are being bet down to 3-1. "I compensate for the increasing difficulty of finding good betting values. Instead of merely looking at the number, the Figure, I look for other factors to stay ahead of the crowd—such as what kind of circumstances were in place to earn that number," Beyer explains.

Even so, he admits, the game is becoming increasingly difficult to beat. "The track used to be the place to play a lucky number. Now there are slots and state lotteries and so forth. So the people who are left are a pretty sophisticated crowd. The margins have shrunk. Still," Beyer says, "with full-card simulcasting, you can find five or six overlays a day. And this game still has one redeeming virtue. You can make huge scores on relatively small investments."

To illustrate his point, Beyer bets a twin trifecta—picking first, second, and third in two consecutive races—in Pimlico's third and fourth. He invests $250 on the two horse (Chocolate Delight) boxed with the one, three, five, and six, giving him 84 winning combinations out of a possible 60,000. "The two horse's last three races have been very good until his last one, where he was lousy. I'm willing to dismiss the results on account of mud that day." Beyer is particularly fond of twin trifecta (or "double triple") bets. In 1990, at the Laurel track in Maryland, he hit one for $195,000. A year later he hit another for $134,000.

On this day the two runs well, as Beyer had hoped. But "an inscrutable performance" from the seven horse, a nag Beyer completely discounted, kills the trifecta chances.

"At heart I'm an exotic bettor," Beyer says. "I get more of a rush. I make some straight bets now and then, or with small exactas, but I prefer to go for the big-paying long shot. I tide myself over with singles and doubles, but I'm really going for the home run."

Such a strategy requires a placid, almost phlegmatic, temperament. Beyer has one. "The worst thing you can let happen to you in betting horses is to be thrown off kilter by emotional highs and lows. You must totally erase close losses and go on," he counsels. "Near misses are an inescapable part of the game."

As his odds-on favorite in the simulcast fourth race at Belmont falters in the stretch, Beyer smiles as if to say, "See what I mean?" He sighs lightly. "Not off to a very auspicious beginning."

At lunch in the clubhouse, Beyer scans his program and announces, "I've got an opinion on the fifth race. This might be the most interesting situation of the day." According to the master handicapper, only three horses (the three, four, and five) of the eight-horse field have any real speed; the others are plodders. Beyer bets a $40 exacta boxed with his three picks. "If two of the three can get the lead from the start, they should run away with the race," he predicts. The four is the favorite; the three and the five, however, are coming off bad races and are paying long odds. If Beyer's analysis is accurate, the payoff should be large. As the horses go to the post, the four goes up to 4-1; the three is bet down to 10-1; and the five is the public's least favorite at 16-1.

Per Beyer's prognostication, the four and five break early and fast, taking a two-length lead by the quarter-pole. "This looks good," Beyer says, nodding.

As they pass the half, the two speed horses have opened a three-length lead and show no sign of tiring. "We're in this one," Beyer says. "We've definitely got a shot. This is the scenario I had hoped for."

As the ponies make the turn toward home, a pack begins to gain ground, but it's essentially a three-horse race: Beyer's four and five, and the pesky one, which is making a late stretch drive. Proving he's human, Andy Beyer, the composed, intellectual, numbers guy without much visual acumen, stares at the charging horses and begins to hum nervously, emitting a high-pitched tone, like a puppy quivering with anticipation.

As the horses approach the wire he can contain himself no longer. "Four-five! Four-five! Four-five! Stay right there! Die right there!"

The horses cross the finish line in a tight pack. But the results are clear: the five by a neck. And in second, the four.

"Yes!" Beyer whoops, slapping high-fives. "Yes!"

He checks the tote board. The exacta pays $162 for a $2 bet. Beyer's ticket is worth more than $3,200.

For about 30 seconds.

The track announcer instructs the bettors to "hold all tickets." There's been a steward's inquiry—and it involves the five horse.

"I'm a jockey hater," Beyer grumbles. "No professional athletes have as poor a tactical understanding of their sport. The guy on the horse's back has no concept of your perfect diagnosis of a race. All he can do is sabotage you, which I'm afraid is about to happen."

82

After an excruciating 10-minute examination of the race tapes, the stewards conclude that the five horse swerved off its line near the finish, blocking the path of the charging one. The five is disqualified.

"Damn," Beyer says quietly. "That would have made our day."

He does not fume long, near misses being an inescapable part of the game. There are other races to look at, other opportunities to consider. To Andrew Beyer, one day at the track does not make or break him; it's all one long gamble.

He begins to assess the next race when an adorable little girl, perhaps six or seven, costumed in a print dress and bonnet, approaches Beyer's table, presents a racing program, and politely asks for his autograph.

"For my daddy," she says, shyly. "He says you're the best."

9

Go, Greyhound!

I start by calling some of my wiseguy pals in Vegas. I tell 'em I'm going to the dog track. I've never bet the dogs before and could certainly use some good advice. My gambling buddies give me a range of responses. Their wisdom runs from "What, are you nuts? You might as well bet on professional wrestling!" to "I've got some powerful methods for betting the hounds, but trust me, they're too complicated to explain on the phone."

Not only do I not know how to handicap a greyhound race, I don't even know the best place to go to bet on the cruising canines. I've heard Alabama has a bunch of tracks. Texas, too.

I ask my friend Paddy, a big-time Vegas sharpie, if there's anything like a Churchill Downs of dog racing. A shrine to the sport. That sort of thing.

He laughs as if I just told him that limerick about the man from Nantucket. "Uh, no," Paddy says. "Dog tracks are dog tracks."

So I go to Miami, where there's dog racing seven days a week, sometimes twice a day. Though you might not be able to get the city fathers to admit it, Miami is a big dog-racing town. Whereas most cities don't have a single dog track to brighten their civic outlook, Miami has two. Drive on the highways and you'll see directional signs with the silhouette of a greyhound in stride, pointing you to the promised land.

Minutes from Miami International Airport is "Fabulous" Flagler Dog Track. I don't know why the fabulous part got added to the name, but whatever once inspired that commendation has long since been forgotten. Flagler, like my friend Paddy suggested, is a dog track. But that's all right, because a dog track is exactly what I'm looking for.

I show up just as the sun is beginning to set, early enough to catch the last of the simulcast races from Denver. I park in valet, because I'm fancying myself a real sport tonight, and more important, it costs only $2. The small crowd hanging around the air-conditioned clubhouse is, like the surrounding neighborhood, a decidedly downmarket bunch. My kind of people. They yell at the television monitors and curse in Spanish and look like they haven't slept in three days. And they probably can't imagine wanting to be anywhere else.

I look around the joint. It's like a horse track, only smaller. Horse tracks have infields big enough to build a golf course. Dog tracks have infields barely big enough to hold a decent softball game. Horse tracks are mint juleps and big lace hats. Dog tracks are plastic cups of Bud and Miami Heat tank tops.

With about an hour until post time, I find an empty spot at one of the clubhouse desks and look over the racing form, pretending I know what I'm doing. The form looks like what you'd get at a horse track, with all sorts of numbers and times that mean nothing to me. I stare at them anyway, like all the other astute handicappers in my midst. Let's face it: Even if you do have some idea of how to separate the champs from the mongrels, you've got to be something of a degenerate to gamble at a dog track. The house take-out (or "vig") is a healthy 17.6% on straight win, place, and show bets, and as high as 24% on exotics. (They post these numbers at all the entrances, so nobody can claim he was bamboozled.) Compare this to a house edge of slightly less than

1% on most blackjack games and you understand what kind of hole you've got to paw yourself out of when you bet the hounds. You gotta be nuts. Or very very sharp.

I've got one wiseguy pal who claims the dogs are eminently more beatable than the horses, because there's no human on their back to influence the race. The dogs run unencumbered and uncoached—except for one glorious moment down in Tijuana, when some Barnum-like track operator got the bright idea of putting monkeys on the dogs' backs.

My sharpie pal tells me his most successful scheme for beating the dogs is "backclassing," betting hounds that are moving down in class, going from strong competition to weak. "Yeah, but doesn't everybody have that information?" I ask him.

"Course they do," he says. "But most of these fools are too busy picking dogs by their names to give a damn."

Now, I take offense at this comment, since I've often found the handicapping-by-name method to be, if not particularly successful, enormously fun. Unscientific, yes. But any less effective than throwing darts? Picking the "lightest" dog in the field? Or betting on the hound with the biggest ass muscles? We'll see.

As I scan the program, making my preliminary selections, I figure I should also go down to the kennel area and take a peek at the competitors. This is my theory: Since my mutt back home, Ella, is half greyhound, I just may be one of those naturals, one of those doggie savants who can simply pick winners by eye. I'm used to looking at a hound—okay, a half-hound—all day. So maybe I've unconsciously learned to recognize a speedy canine. A stretch, I know, but desperate gamblers do desperate things. I take a peek at the holding pen, where dozens of hounds stand around looking bored, and I don't see anything in any of them that makes me want to invest a dime. All I want to do is pet them.

Whether you win or lose, you've got to love the atmosphere at the dog track: The guy behind me is rooting on the hounds *and* making football bets on a cell phone. The guy in front of me is compulsively snapping his fingers, as if shaking out a match, rooting home his favorite dogs—*on taped replays.*

As the hounds are loaded into the starting boxes for the first race, I make my first bet, $2, the minimum, on Simplee Cash. This is a dog that ran in C-class for three of his past four races, running in the D-class tonight. *Backclassing,* I think, remembering my sharpie pal's handicapping advice. I'm planning to lose this race, planning on just getting my feet wet and all that. So is it any wonder I'm laughing like an under-medicated mental patient when Simplee Cash leads wire-to-wire and wins by a lean, muscular eight lengths? I'm up eleven bucks and I haven't even figured out where I want to sit, yet.

There are two schools of thought on this issue. The first is: Watch them from up in the clubhouse, where you can see agonizing replays of your mutt getting nipped in a photo finish, and where cute Latina waitresses bring you drinks and snacks. The second option: Go down in front of the grandstand, yards from where the handlers parade the hounds. This is a prime location to get all sorts of useless tips from old disheveled men in food-stained shirts.

I try both. Down near the track, one of the wiseguys points at a dog about to run the second race and says to me, "You see that pup? You see her? Let me tell you something. That pup's got moxie!" Personally, I like the perspective from the Flagler clubhouse because it sits high above the first turn, where the dogs frequently wipe out, making great piles of toppled fur.

My next round of bets is a pure name play. I plunk down half my profits on Tammy's Connie, in honor of my friend Tammy, and Nora's Big Red, in honor of her red hair. At the last minute I bet some more on another dog—one with no recognizable name value—after I hear some clever-looking types whispering conspiratorially about it. Tammy, Red, and the hot tip finish well back in the pack, sniffing the winner's tail the entire race.

Undaunted, I make another name play, Yasou Mike, because, hey, I'm Mike! I bet him with another pup who's moving down in class. I also make a win bet on the lightest hound in the race, just to try that particular bit of time-tested wizardry. With what's left of my winnings I tip the nice ticket lady, who calls me "honey." My smile is meant to suggest to her, *"You can afford to be a sport when you know how to pick 'em, darlin'."* (Hey, if you don't know what you're doing, at least swagger like you do.) To my delight, the lightweight breaks quickly and holds off a late charge to win, paying close to $21. Naturally, I'm feeling like some sort of greyhound genius.

Of course, authentic dog-track geniuses probably don't giggle as much as I do. But I can't help it. I'm feeling happy and silly and strangely invincible. Besides, the dogs themselves are pretty funny too, the way they bob up and down the track, chasing a rag on a motorized stick. Thoroughbred horses have a majestic power about them as they charge down the homestretch; the dogs just look goofy. It's mostly the plastic muzzles they wear, which are primarily meant to prevent them from biting each other, but also, I suspect, serve the noble purpose of discouraging the hounds from laying down in the middle of a race and licking their scrotums.

My on-paper pick for the fourth race, How About You (a great jazz standard), turns out to look a lot like my own pup Ella, so she's a natural lock. She's also the second lightest pup in the race and moving down in class. Most important, I can swear she winks at me as she heads toward the starting line. Swimming in luck-begotten profits, I "box" her (bet all possible combinations) with two other backclassers, the one and the four, just to keep my absent wiseguy friend placated. Strangely, once the race begins, How About You is nowhere to be seen—probably too busy winking at other guys. But the one and the four do their backclass thing and torch the field, returning a monstrous $84 for a $2 wager.

I let out a triumphant whoop.

"You had those dogs?" another gambler asks, incredulously.

"Oh, yeah," I say nonchalantly.

"You're pretty hot," he says, smiling.

"On fire, my friend," I say, nodding like an idiot. "Smoking."

Regrettably, for the fifth, sixth, and seventh races, my flame goes out. As they say, I can't pick my mother out of a police line-up.

I bet a bundle on a pup named Mr. Connick—a sure-thing name play, despite the fact he's a 50-1 shot.

No sweet music.

I bet a bundle on a pup named Cool Christi, since that's the name of one of my editors.

Rewrite!

I bet a bundle on two other hounds moving way down in class. After their miserable performances, they're probably still moving down.

Despite my frigid streak, I'm still up for the night. Better yet, I've managed to flirt a few times with a terribly sexy waitress named Melina, who pronounces the "ch" in "chef salad" like she's saying "chutney." I'm in love.

Momentarily distracted by thoughts of sharing dog stories with Melina over cocktails, I absentmindedly pick two dogs in the eighth without even looking at their names. Backclassing and all that. *Where's that waitress?* Strong finishes their last two races. *I've got to tell her how beautiful she is.* Whatever.

The two pups come in 1-2, and I'm $25 richer.

The next time Melina comes by, I spring this super suave line on her: "What's a beautiful woman like you doing working at a dog track?"

She stares at me blankly.

"I mean..." *Whoops.* I explain I've never been to a dog track before, and it's, well, you know, not necessarily dripping with class, and...

"It's only part-time," Melina says icily. "You want another drink?"

I suggest we have one together, after she's done with work. She tells me "no" in about 32 different ways before I get the message.

For the next few races the dogs ignore me as blithely as Melina. I pick three hounds to finish 1-2-3; they come in 6-7-8. I bet on a pup to win; he straggles in second. I gamble on the lightest dog; the heaviest wins by a mile. Finally, I find a greyhound I can believe in: Headline Hunter. I feel a connection, a spiritual thing. This dog has been put here at Flagler expressly for me to bet on him. I make my biggest dog track wager ever, $20, and along with all the other gamblers I scream my brains out rooting him home.

He loses, of course. By about 10 lengths.

It's nearly midnight. There's one race to go. One shot at redemption. My theory is if Melina won't favor me with her charms, maybe Lady Luck will. Lucky in cards, unlucky in love, and vice versa. That's my thinking.

I find a dog called Where's Renee, which is similar to my mom's name. The concept here is: Hey, if all the pretty girls scorn you, there's always mom. This may be too Oedipal for some, but all I know is it works—at least in dog racing. My hound breaks well from the box, survives a late rush from the outside, and brings home a $28 winning ticket. Redemption, thy name is Where's Renee!

The waitress has vanished. All my betting buddies are drifting away into the Miami night. I'm alone at my clubhouse desk, surrounded by losing betting slips and empty cups, staring out at the now deserted track.

"You get lucky tonight?" one old-timer asks me, on his way toward the exit.

"Well…" I say, pausing to decide how much irony this fellow will be able to handle at this hour.

"Yeah, I know, pal," he says, shaking his head. "I know. Them dogs will break your heart." He rips a ticket in half and tosses it over his shoulder. It flutters to the floor as he shuffles away.

On the
Golf Course

10

The World's Greatest
Golf Hustler

He has probably won more money playing golf than anyone in the history of the sport. More than Jack Nicklaus. More than Tom Kite. Even more than Greg Norman, the sport's all-time leading official money-winner with more than $10 million in tournament earnings.

The game of golf has been surpassingly good to Terrance Leon Jr. Thanks to his victories on the links he has his own private jet and a sprawling 6,000-square-foot mansion in upstate New York; he has a fleet of luxury automobiles in his six-car garage; he even has his own golf learning center in the basement, fully outfitted with video cameras and swing-analyzing computers and all manners of techno-gadgetry. Thanks to his exploits on the golf course Terrance Leon Jr. has all the trappings of wealth that accompany the wildly successful and the famous.

Only you've never heard of Terrance Leon Jr. He doesn't endorse golf balls or have his own line of sportswear. He's never won a major championship. Indeed, he's never even played in a professional golf tournament. If you were to see him hitting balls at your local practice range, you wouldn't recognize his face, nor would you be able to identify his peculiar golf swing as you would, say, that of Fred Couples or Nick Price.

No, Terrance Leon Jr. is a cipher, a man who lives in the

shadows not the spotlight. He's anonymous. And he likes it that way. For that's about the only way a man in his line of work can run his business.

Terrance Leon Jr. is the world's greatest golf hustler.

* * *

"I grew up dirt poor," he says, stroking towering wedge shots on the practice range of a famous golf course in south Florida. "We lived in a small town in Tennessee, about four-teen-hundred people. No indoor toilet facilities, four kids to one bedroom—it was tough." The memory does not seem to pain him so much as amuse him. "Even as a little boy, seven or eight, I knew I was going to be something. Just didn't know it was going to be a gambler."

His voice is still thick and slow, like apricot nectar. He still has the courtly manners of a southern gentleman. But Terrance Leon Jr.'s coal-black eyes are not those of a country hick who has somehow wandered awestruck into the big city. They're the eyes of a cold calculating killer, the eyes of someone who refuses to lose at anything.

"I was introduced to gambling as a youngster. I grew up around pool tables and games of marbles, and from the start I enjoyed the competition. And I enjoyed coming away with more than I started with. Course, I wasn't very good as a kid. Shoot, I'd bet on anything, just to gamble. As a ten-year-old I bet the grocer on the World Series, Yankees versus Dodgers, and I lost all my paper-route money. Hell, I just loved the action."

As a teenager Leon worked "here and there" at factory and foundry jobs. "But that wasn't for me," he says. "I was already making more money shooting pool than I could ever make punching the time clock. Almost from the start I was a successful gambler. Only problem was I couldn't hold on to my money. I couldn't manage it right. I'd win eighty thousand playing nine-ball and turn right around and blow a hundred thousand on horses and sports. This went on for years."

Eventually, Leon decided to treat his gambling not as an addiction but a business. "That's what's made all the difference. Gambling stopped being fun and it started being a way to make a living. I figured I wasn't going to get involved in nothing unless I was getting the best of it. If I didn't have the advantage, I wouldn't play. That's the secret. Find something where you're getting the best of the deal and stick with it till there ain't no money left to win."

Leon was not, by his own admission, much of a golf player in his early days. Like anyone who takes up the world's most frustrating game, he initially struggled with golf, losing thousands of dollars in bad bets in the process. "Hell, I couldn't break ninety and I'm playing guys for five grand! But I knew one day I'd come back and beat those same guys for ten times as much. That's the great thing about golf," he says, peppering a flagstick 160 yards down the range. "Nobody can stop you from shooting a good score. You're competing against yourself and the golf course. I decided I was never going to let me beat me."

In one year, practicing 80 hours a week, Leon went from an 18 handicap to a 6. A year later he was down to a 3 handicap. And a year after that he was playing at scratch—a level of accomplishment he maintains today, nearly three decades later. Watching him play a "casual" (for a meager $3,000) 36 holes, one realizes Terrance Leon Jr., in fact, has the kind of golf game that could easily dominate the Senior PGA Tour: He's monstrously long off the tee, surgically precise with his irons, and possesses a short game worthy of Phil Mickelson. The man, shall we say, can *play.*

But being able to shoot low scores is not the key to being the world's greatest golf hustler.

"You want to win money on the golf course?" he asks rhetorically, lining up a short birdie putt. "You got to get your opponents out of their element and into your element. Sure, you got to have some ability, but it's more important how you react under pressure. Playing for fifty bucks, guy might shoot the grass off the course. But playing for two hundred, that same guy might not be able to break a hundred and ten. On the other hand," he says, calmly sinking his putt, "some guys get *better* the higher the stakes."

He smiles. "I'll tell you a story."

Several years ago Leon heard from a friend in the entertainment business that a certain television action star—one of the biggest celebrities of the late '80s—was looking to play some big-money golf matches. The television star wasn't a particularly good player—he'd broken 90 only a few times in his life—but given enough strokes he would play for "a whole bunch of money." With no guarantees of a match, only the faint promise that the star would consider any "reasonable offer," Leon flew to Maui where the star kept one of his many vacation homes. After checking into a hotel, Leon went straight to the golf course to evaluate his prey.

"The guy wasn't as bad as some people had told me he was. But he also wasn't as good as *he* thought he was," Leon recalls. "I figured I'd take a shot. If he beat me once I was going to quit him. But I felt somehow that wasn't going to happen. No, sir, I was going to make sure of that."

The art of Leon's business is not, he claims, being able to hit 300-yard drives and hole every bunker shot. "Sure, you got to be able to play some," he says. "But what I do is all about negotiating and evaluating. I've always been pretty good at matching up. Learning how to make a good match is ninety percent of the game."

Leon offered the star what seemed to be a generous offer: 18 shots in match play and 22 shots in medal play. The medal-play bet was for $25,000. The match-play bet was a $50,000 Nassau, in which the players compete for three separate prizes: the front nine, the back nine, and the overall.

Leon beat the star 31 days in a row for well over $3 million.

How, any reasonable person might wonder, did Leon get the star to continue playing after he'd lost even three or four times in a row? "Well, I didn't have to get him to do anything. He *wanted* to play. Twenty-five out of thirty-one of those times this guy had the advantage going into the fifteenth hole. I mean, he had me beat. All he had to do was shoot triple-bogeys coming in and he'd get the money."

Incredibly, as Leon and his caddie tried mightily not to laugh out loud, the star consistently shot 10s, 13s, even 18s when the pressure became intense.

"He kept playing because he knew he should have been winning. On paper he had way the best of it," Leon explains. "But this is the key to gambling at golf: The winner is immune to pressure. He can always play to his ability. The loser can't."

Leon smiles faintly. "I've always been able to."

The world's greatest golf hustler does not attempt to disguise his talent—anyone who watches him swing a golf club immediately recognizes the man can play. His success, he says, is not the product of looking bad on the practice range and beautiful on the golf course; it's not the product of making intentionally unorthodox swings that look like they've been constructed in a tool shed (à la Lee Trevino), then shooting the lights out. He's the best in the business because when he gets nervous his game does not deteriorate. It gets better.

"I play a match for chicken feed and I don't do so well," Leon admits. "But when we're playing for something substantial, it makes me more focused, more intense. In a big match I probably play *better* than my abilities."

Terrance Leon Jr. has played thousands of matches for tens of millions of dollars. But perhaps no single game was ever bigger than one he had with the CEO of a Texas-based oil company. "I met this fellow—we'll call him 'the Chairman'—in Las Vegas, at the old Dunes golf course," Leon remembers. "This man was successful at everything he did. His entire life was one victory after another. The man had no fear. There was virtually no amount of money we wouldn't play for. Which was fine, 'cause that's basically been my policy my entire career."

In Las Vegas, the Chairman played the Hustler in a "friendly" match for $50,000. Leon lost. "Not intentionally, mind you," he says, half seriously. "I was giving him a few too many strokes. But the gentleman played great. And naturally, I took every opportunity to remind him of that fact."

Flush with victory, the Chairman invited Leon to play in Austin, Texas, at the Chairman's home course. "We'll play for whatever you want," the Chairman told Leon. "Even up."

The Chairman was about a 4 handicap. The Hustler was scratch. "I liked my chances," Leon says, strolling to the 18th tee box.

The first nine they played, Leon beat the oilman out of $120,000. The next nine, The Chairman pressed his bets and lost $240,000. To Leon's delight, his opponent suggested they play again the next morning, double or nothing. "Funny thing about that match. I hadn't really played all that well the first day. Shot like a seventy-three," Leon recalls. "So even though I was playing for a quarter million the next day, I wasn't too concerned. I knew I could only play better."

He did, posting a 69 on a course he had seen only twice before. The Chairman wrote Leon a check for $480,000. "That was about my best day on the golf course," Leon says, striping his drive down the middle of the fairway. "Made about thirty-five grand per shot."

Leon's record against what he calls "very good players" is stellar. In fact, against the players we watch on television every weekend, he claims he's "hardly ever lost." Indeed, professional golfers, Leon reveals, are usually his favorite opponents. "I'm much more fearful of a seasoned gambler than a touring pro," Leon says, lining up an 8-iron approach shot. "There's a huge difference, I mean a world of difference, playing for some sponsor's prize money and playing for money that you have to reach into your own back pocket for."

Most professionals, whose skill level is, admittedly, far greater than even the best amateurs, tend to wilt under what Terrance Leon Jr. calls "real heat." "Without exception, the pros underestimate me and overestimate themselves. And when there comes a point in the match where they realize they might just have to pay off a real big number, well, they change. Gambling to them is a hundred-dollar Nassau. A really big match, a huge match, would be something like five thousand. For me, I don't even really start paying attention until fifty thousand or so."

Among the name-brand professionals whom Leon admires, the ones he believes can play for their own money, are Raymond Floyd and Lee Trevino. "So can Jim Colbert," he says, lacing his iron to within 10 feet of the pin. "But most of them..." he shrugs dismissively.

"I'll tell you another story," he says.

Several years ago Terrance Leon Jr. played a very talented gentleman in a two-day match. So talented was this nice gentleman that he agreed to give his opponent two strokes per side—and ended up owing Leon $18,000. He paid the Hustler promptly, half in cash and half in check. Leon never cashed the check. Instead, he framed it.

Leon likes telling this story not because of the money involved. It's one of his favorites, because the nice gentleman is one of the few men walking the planet to have won both the U.S. Open and the Masters. "Every time I see this guy on television," Leon says, "I think to myself what a nice gentleman he is."

Lately, Terrance Leon Jr. has been devoting more time to a portfolio of business interests than to the golf course. The Senior Tour, he says, would be a challenge, a "great chase," but besides the constant travel, there's not enough money in it to keep him interested. "I plan to enter a few tournaments, anyway," Leon says. "Just to compete and meet some nice people. That's all I want out of golf these days. Before, it was all about money. Now I realize anyone who plays and enjoys golf and enjoys the people he's with is a big winner, no matter what he does or doesn't accomplish."

Still, he says, he has one big golfing goal. In a couple of years he'd like to fulfill a lifelong dream and play in the U.S. Senior Amateur, which, should he win it, surely would be one of the most ironic titles ever bestowed.

"Yes, I suppose I fall somewhere between a professional and an amateur. An amateur is, well, an amateur. And a professional is someone who plays for a living. I've been successful enough that I don't really have to do that anymore," Terrance Leon Jr. says.

"On the other hand, if anyone's looking for a big game," he says, smiling, "I'm available."

11

The Ultimate Comp

Andre Agassi is off playing the U.S. Open tennis tournament, so I know he won't mind me sitting in front of his locker while I change into golf shoes.

Of course, I could have used the locker of any number of absent hackers: Bill Gates, busy swallowing up Apple; Kevin Costner, Bruce Willis, and Will Smith, shooting movies that many people will actually pay to see; Phil Mickelson, Mark O'Meara, and Ray Floyd, PGA-Touring the country in search of fairways and greens; George Bush, yipping putts in Kennebunkport.

Good thing I didn't appropriate Michael Jordan's space, though—shortly after I start to lace my shoes, Michael Jordan himself strolls over to his locker, dispensing "howya doins" and "hey, whazzups" to the awestruck mortals he leaves in his wake.

Welcome to Shadow Creek.

Here are the ground rules: You are perfectly welcome here—for about five hours or so, or however long it takes you to play golf, have lunch, and purchase pro-shop memorabilia to show your jealous friends back home. Then please go quietly. And don't bug Michael while you're on the premises.

* * *

There's a not-altogether-new concept sweeping American golf. It's called "high-end daily fee" or "country club for a day." The idea is to give customers all the trappings of a country club experience—the gracious attendants, the comfortable clubhouse, the immaculate golf course—without some of the more niggling details of actually belonging to a country club. Like $50,000 initiation fees, for starters. Greens fees at country-club-for-a-day courses often surpass $100. But given the lavish "yes sir!" service, along with putting surfaces that do what few municipal versions can (that is, provide a smooth roll), nobody questions if the hefty tariff is worth it. Of course it's worth it! You're playing golf on a real golf course. And everything is just so.

Shadow Creek redefines the phrase high-end daily fee. A day here costs $1,000.

* * *

In 1989, Mirage Resorts, the company that owns such Las Vegas casinos as the Golden Nugget, Treasure Island, and the Mirage, built a golf course in the middle of an otherwise unoccupied tract of barren North Las Vegas desolation. Since the absence of topography, trees, grass, animals, and any other sign of life does not generally make for a pleasant day on the links, the Mirage people hired the renowned architect Tom Fazio, brought in enough earth-moving equipment to rebuild the Panama Canal, and spent something like $40 million to transform complete nothingness into the lushest golf course in the world.

Shadow Creek was instantly hailed as the finest new private golf course in America and accorded top-10 status in all the golf magazine beauty pageants. It had the wide rolling fairways of Augusta, the mature pines of the North Carolina sand hills, and the kind of achingly beautiful landscaping normally seen only on the grounds of better European castles. All manner of exotic birds roamed the course's ponds and brooks. The turf was an unblemished emerald carpet, devoid of cactus and tumbleweed and any other unsightly distraction that might remind players they were in the heart of the Mojave Desert. And the clubhouse grill served fresh lobster.

Or so most of the golfing public believed. No one—well, almost no one—had actually *played* the golf course.

Unlike visiting, say, Cypress Point or Winged Foot, two fortresses of supposed exclusivity, you couldn't get a member to take you. That's because Shadow Creek had only one member, Steve Wynn, the swashbuckling chairman of Mirage Resorts, whose mansion (one of only two homes on the course) overlooks the 18th fairway. The only way to play Shadow Creek was to receive an invitation, and these were reserved for an elite minority: friends of the corporation, management employees, and most important, "premium" casino customers.

In gambling parlance, *premium customers* means high rollers who lose a lot of money. Casinos court these valuable contributors to the bottom line with lavish perquisites known as "comps" (complimentaries), such as gourmet meals, hotel suites, stretch limousines, and ringside fight tickets—all on the house. To dissuade a premium loser from taking his action elsewhere, the casinos are constantly upgrading their comps, offering more luxury, more pampering, more coddling. To distinguish its largesse from the competition's, the Mirage had the brilliant idea of offering its best customers the most private, most exclusive, most sublime golf experience in the world, where only the anointed few—the loftiest of the high rollers—could play in undisturbed bliss, in a tropical wonderland, amid pheasants and swans and wallabies.

Shadow Creek would be the ultimate comp.

From a business standpoint, the strategy worked magnificently. Those who golf have an unhealthy compulsion to dig up sod where most others haven't. Getting to play an Augusta, a Pine Valley, or even your local town's "best" course is a hacker's badge of honor. (It makes us feel special, even if our golf swings aren't.) Heavy hitters from around the globe flocked to the Mirage, hoping to be among the first, the few, to play Shadow Creek. Within a few months, the golf course's outlandish construction costs were completely paid for by several golf-crazy gamblers, including the notorious Ken Mizuno, whose multi-million-dollar losses at the baccarat table presaged his imprisonment for land fraud, but earned him unlimited play on the secret links.

Gaining access to Shadow Creek had nothing to do with knowing the right people or being the right religion or having a fat bank account. And being a golf journalist didn't help either. "By prohibiting any media on the course, it allowed us to maintain an aura of mystique," says Alan Feldman, Mirage Resorts vice president of public affairs. "Since gaining access to the course wasn't connected to magazines or television, we didn't want to build expectations that we couldn't fulfill. So we had to learn to say 'no' to a lot of people."

I was one of them. Several years ago Mr. Feldman politely hit me with the *"thank you for your interest, but please stay far away"* policy. But now, eight years after Shadow Creek opened its wrought-iron gates, that's all changing.

* * *

Here's the Shadow Creek deal: For $1,000, a guest may purchase one of 6 to 12 tee times available for purchase each day. (Availability is contingent on the number of invited guests; midweek is best.) The fee includes a caddie to escort you around the 6,701-yard (from the men's tees), par-72 layout; round-trip limousine transportation to and from the club; and a suite at the Mirage, Treasure Island, or Golden Nugget. One other player, staying in the same suite, may participate for an additional $500.

"It's like pricing jewelry," Alan Feldman says. "There's some intrinsic value. But you mostly have to consider the artistic elements." In this case, you get to play the most exclusive golf course on the planet, while Michael Jordan snap-hooks his drives in the foursome ahead of you.

Allowing any hacker with a credit card to play Shadow Creek is akin to golf's Berlin Wall coming down. But, as accountants sometimes say, the golf course had a "higher best use." Like actually being used.

"We had a problem," Armen Suny, Shadow Creek's general manager, says. "We were too slow. Now, with the new policy, at least we get to see some people." The difference has been dramatic. Suny was forced to *double* the size of his dining-room staff—from one to two.

Still, Shadow Creek retains its sense of intimacy. "We realized we can never dilute the experience," Feldman says. "We don't have any more play than before—our limit is only twelve to twenty foursomes a day—just a slightly different mix of players."

Now hackers like you and me can follow in the divot marks of the rich and famous and gambling-obsessed. For anyone who has ever suffered the indignities of big-city municipal golf, discovering the pleasures of Shadow Creek is like being supplied with swing tips by the ghost of Ben Hogan.

The suite they install you in at the Mirage is as large as my house, with significantly more furniture and telephones. It's the kind of place where you'd like to throw a party for maybe 40 beautiful and glamorous types, if only you knew that many movie or porn stars. The kind of place where, when room service comes, a waiter sets your dining-room table with linen before leaving behind stuffed artichokes and curried Singaporean noodles. Where it takes 10 minutes to figure out the remote control for the 31-inch televi-sion-VCR-stereo-CD player-rice cooker that sits in an armoire the size of your rental car. It's the kind of place where your companion asks if it would be all right to stay a little longer—like two weeks.

Downstairs, in the health club, you're not at all surprised to run into Dennis Rodman, working out his highly pierced physique, while several accompanying hoochie girls preen in the mirrors. Nor does it shock you to see Michael Jordan and Ahmad Rashad, surrounded by bodyguards, playing blackjack in the heart of the casino.

This is the Mirage: Land of the Blessed. And for a pittance, for a fraction of one of Jordan's Gatorade advertisement royalty checks, you can be an honorary high roller, too.

What's most impressive about the Shadow Creek experience is the golf course. To purists weaned on the "you-can't-top-the-wonder-of-nature" school of golf-course design, Shadow Creek will make you question your architectural hermeneutics. Like Las Vegas itself, no part of the layout is natural; not a single millimeter of the land has been left as it was found. Startling elevation changes, sparkling waterfalls, the eponymous creek that gurgles through the course—all of it is the work of man, but work done so well, so ingeniously, that the hand of man is undetectable. The par 3s, for example, are easily the most beautiful collection of one-shotters I've ever seen. All of them feature carries over immense valleys filled with a variety of rocky chasms, vibrant wetlands, and shimmering flowers. You have to keep reminding yourself that the thrilling vista before you was once as flat and featureless as a casino crap table.

Shadow Creek is not a terribly difficult golf course (remember for whom it was originally designed). It's not a course that wears you out and depletes your stock of golf balls. It's not a place where you curse the golf gods for tricking you into playing such a maddening game. No, Shadow Creek is a fun golf course. It's a course that swaddles you with pleasure. It's a place where you count your blessings, smile broadly, and try desperately not to stare when Michael Jordan shanks one off the first tee.

The
Straight

Dope

The
Straight
Dope

12

New, Different, and Unbeatable

Everyone who loses his money in Vegas has a different reason. For the innocents it's the bright lights and free drinks, the dazzling timelessness of the place, which puts susceptible visitors into a sort of sensory fog, a super-charged fugue state. For compulsive plungers it's the action, the endless opportunities to be in play, whether on a roll of the dice or the turn of a card or even the stride of a greyhound.

But for the vast majority of Vegas victims, most are separated from their money merely because they are either too lazy or too dimwitted to do a little math.

Casinos can be pretty and elegant and faux glamorous. But never forget their primary function: to win your money.

In the pursuit of that goal, the casinos must constantly conjure up new and exciting ways to get a patron to stand still, reach into his wallet, and put his cash into play. This is why, whether you're a frequent visitor to the land of neon or simply a once-a-year reveler in town for a bachelor party, you'll notice a panoply of new and unfamiliar games at which you can try your luck. Some look vaguely like old favorites, some *are* old favorites dressed up in new clothes, and some are like nothing you've ever played.

According to one of the industry's new-game innovators, Bill Burt, director of table games at Harrah's Las Vegas, the casinos have seen a dramatic shift away from table games to slot machines, those buzzing and gurgling short-change artists that retain an opiate hold on their faithful customers. In order to win some of those players back—and to cultivate new players—executives like Burt, a former professional gambler, are constantly searching for fresh games to entice the masses.

"Many of the new games are what we consider 'cross-over' games," he says. "They're designed to interest slot players. To many of these players, table games are too intimidating, too complicated. So the best new games are simple, and they have some of the elements the slot players prefer, like a big progressive jackpot."

Burt says maybe one out of 10 new games makes it in the long run. "The best ones involve concepts the players are already familiar with, games that are based on other games people already play," he explains. "But even when the games are easy to understand, we see, in addition to the house edge, a lot of player inexpertise that contributes to a big hold for the house."

Bill Burt's point is that these new games, while easy to learn, are sometimes difficult to analyze. No matter how earnest and responsible a gambler you fancy yourself, if you can't accurately compute the house edge on these fresh propositions, you'll never know how bad—or how good, in some rare cases—you're getting it.

So here's some help.

Gambling, to the casual player, is entertainment. And the price of admission is the house edge, an almost imperceptible mechanism that allows the house to slowly but surely win the money. The trick is to lower the price of admission, just as you would by taking advantage of a two-for-one movie offer. If you can find a better game or implement a better strategy, you can actually be paid to play.

Are any of the new games worth your time? Here's what I found.

Casino War

Take the ancient children's game of War, put it on a blackjack table, dress it up with a silly proposition bet, and you've got one of the newest—and most inane—table games ever to hit Las Vegas. You make a wager, usually $5 minimum. The dealer gives each player one card face up; he gives himself one card face up. If your card is higher than the dealer's, you win. If it's not, you lose. (Seriously.) The casino has absolutely no advantage on this portion of the game and, as you might imagine, the "battles" are about as interesting as a John Tesh concert. If you like playing "rocks-paper-scissors" for kicks, Casino War is for you.

There's also a "tie" bet, which pays 10-1 and has a staggering 18.65% advantage for your pals in the suits and name tags. Ignore it.

If your initial confrontation with the dealer does result in a tie, you may either surrender your bet or "go to war," in which case you must post another bet equal to your original one. In a move of almost three-card-monte-like finesse, the dealer posts a chip, appearing to "match" your second bet. He doesn't, however, match your first bet. In effect, you're betting two chips to win one every time you go to war. This is where the casino gains its overall house edge.

Forget pacifism. The optimal strategy is never surrender—always go to war. Surrendering gives the casino a 3.7% advantage. Going to war is only 2.88%. And, of course, never take the tie proposition.

It's not unusual to see suckers wagering large amounts on this simpleton's game, trying to get on a hot streak. Unless you're like the sophisticated team of shuffle-trackers who figured out a powerful strategy for following the high cards through the mixing process (and briefly won a pile of money before the casinos caught on), I wouldn't recommend it. If you're curious—and you might be for about two minutes—try to find a full table with a good-looking dealer and treat it as a social event, not as a serious gamble.

Caribbean Stud Poker

This game, in which the player tries to make a five-card poker hand higher than the dealer's, has become immensely popular with casual gamblers for one reason: a progressive jackpot that sometimes tops $100,000. To win the jackpot, you must post a $1 side bet—and be dealt a royal flush. This happens approximately one out of every 648,000 hands, or once every 11,000 hours.

The progressive bet is a big loser. To make the jackpot proposition even remotely playable, you'll have to find a meter that's around $300,000. In a recent informal survey, I found most Las Vegas Caribbean Stud meters set between $28,000 and $72,000.

The basic bet in Caribbean Stud—usually a $5 minimum—is called the "ante bet," which buys you five cards and a peek at one of the dealer's cards. If you like your hand—that is, you think it will beat the dealer's hand—you may "raise," doubling your ante bet. Experts suggest raising with A-K-J-8-3 or better, including any pair, no matter how low. Even following this strategy perfectly, you'll be fading a 5.3% disadvantage on the ante bet, remarkably close to roulette, one of the most larcenous games in the casino.

There are additional levels of strategy variations involving the suit of the dealer's up-card that, if you apply them perfectly, will net you an additional .00000025% gain, which means that you would have to put $4 million in play to capture 1¢ of saving.

The only way to beat Caribbean Stud is to collude with your playing partners, sharing information on the cards in your hands. Assuming you were a "super-colluder," as gambling mathematician Peter Griffin calls them, able to collect and process this information perfectly, you would hold a 2.3% edge over the house. Unfortunately, flashing cards to others at the table is not allowed.

Until the casinos change this rule—and they never will—I suggest finding the highest jackpot meter in town, making the game a social event with your buddies, and enjoying the free drinks.

Let It Ride

The house edge on the $1 side bet that qualifies players for the jackpot is a stupendous 47%. Which is another way of saying that for every $1 you bet chasing the jackpot, you can expect to get 53¢ back.

The game has a flashy sign and a loud musical soundtrack that gets triggered whenever someone hits a big winner. But the real innovation with Let It Ride, the aspect that's captured the imagination of the gambling public, is the fact that you can pull back two out of the three bets you make. People feel like they're getting a great deal, a refund, even though they're not.

Players place three equal wagers on a modified black-jack table—plus that nefarious $1 jackpot bet. The dealer distributes three cards to each player. If you don't like your cards, you may pull back one of your three wagers. The dealer reveals a common card, face up on the table. If you don't like your four-card poker hand, you may pull back another wager. Then the dealer turns over a fifth card, com-pleting your poker hand. If you make a pair of 10s or better, you win.

A gambling writer named Stanley Ko has determined that the perfect strategy for this game is to pull back all bets on non-winners, except on certain suited straight and flush draws. But even if you play perfectly, the house has a 3.5% advantage on the basic bet and the astronomical advantage on the jackpot bet. Since three out of four hands are losers, I suggest looking for a crowded table and, again, making a social event out of it. Sure, lightning can strike. But if you play Let It Ride for any reason other than fun—if, for in-stance, you think you can beat it—you're nuts.

Spanish 21

The casino's promotional literature promises Spanish 21 is the "Same old game. Great new rules." Great if you're the casino.

Spanish 21, in fact, is almost *exactly* like old-fashioned

blackjack, except the player's blackjack beats the dealer's blackjack and the player's 21 beats the dealer's 21; you may re-split aces and hit them multiple times; you may double on any total or any number of cards; if you don't like the results of your double, you may "rescue" your double-down bet and surrender your original; and certain hands (five-, six-, and seven-card 21s, for example) pay small bonuses. There's also a "super jackpot," awarded when a player holds three suited 7s *and* the dealer has a 7 up.

Sounds terrific. There's only one catch: The 10s are removed from the deck, reducing the pack to 48 cards and boosting the casino's off-the-top edge to about 2.5%.

Even with all the weird rules, Spanish 21 is slightly worse than any regular blackjack game you can find on the Las Vegas Strip. If you play this game perfectly, making all sorts of complicated strategy adjustments to account for the esoteric rules—and, believe me, almost no one plays this game perfectly—the house still has about a .8% edge. Keep in mind, the worst Las Vegas blackjack game with terrible rules is still only a .5% advantage for the casino against perfect play.

If you insist on playing Spanish 21, experts recommend never taking insurance, hitting more of your low "stiff" totals (12s, 13s, 14s) when the dealer shows 2-6, and using the rescue feature when the dealer shows 8 through ace and you're stiff. Still, with all the beatable blackjack around, it's crazy to play this game. The jackpot has virtually no value. It's strictly for adrenalin junkies who want to get more action, but in worse circumstances than traditional 21. It's a mystery to me why people like Spanish 21. Learn basic strategy, find a standard single-deck blackjack game, and you'll be a lot better off.

10/7 Double Bonus Poker

Though it's not a table game, this new version of video poker is worth your attention. When played perfectly, the game returns 100.17%. That's right: The player actually has the edge over the house. (Another game, full-pay "deuces wild," returns 100.7%. But it's often hard to find unoccupied machines, since video poker pros latch onto these games like barnacles.)

Don't be fooled by impostors like bonus poker or double double bonus or double bonus deluxe. These games have diminished pay scales that return less to the player. Find a machine that's marked double bonus poker, where the pay table indicates that, with a single coin played, a full house pays 10 units and a flush pays seven units. A strategy chart can teach you the correct plays. And even if you just employ the same strategy you would use on a standard jacks or better video poker machine, you'll still get a 99.7% return. Combine that with a slot club rebate and you've got the best of it.

Russian Roulette

One noted Las Vegas casino recently unveiled a new game called Russian Roulette. As its name implies, early analysis suggested this blackjack-style game may be potentially fatal. Further study pegged the casino advantage to be 9%.

Apparently the public's appetite for self-flagellation wasn't as large as the casinos presumed. Russian Roulette didn't last.

13

The Best and
the Worst

A funny thing happens to passengers on airline flights into Las Vegas. They get gripped with Gambling Fever.

The symptoms are similar to what happens to pre-teen children as the car they're riding in gets within eyesight of an amusement park: excess nervous energy, manifested primarily by incessant wiggling of the feet and pumping of the knees; an increased heart rate, manifested by loud involuntary laughter; and most telling, a sudden non-fatal loss of good sense. For those stricken with the most virulent strains of Gambling Fever, this last symptom usually takes the form of authoritative—but completely incoherent—dissertations on betting systems, wagering tricks, and other "fool-proof" schemes to win at otherwise unwinnable casino games.

On most of these Vegas-bound flights, the nonsensical chattering starts up about 20 minutes before landing, just as the airplane begins its initial descent. But in extreme cases, the ranting has been known to commence even as the flight is taxiing to the runway for take-off. On trans-continental journeys, the gibberish can last for up to five hours, causing nausea, irritability, and temporary insanity in any reasonable person within earshot.

For example, on a recent flight to Las Vegas, one could have overheard the following conversation between a character we'll call the Expert, a suave well-dressed older man wearing a diamond pinkie ring, and the Student, an attractive, much younger woman sitting across the aisle.

Expert: You gamble much in Vegas?

Student: Of course. I love it!

Expert: What games do you like?

Student: I play the slots a little. But I mostly play blackjack.

Expert: Oh, you shouldn't do that. Blackjack is the game where the house has the biggest advantage.

Student: Really?

Expert: Oh, sure. You're better off playing Caribbean Stud poker. Much better.

Student (wide-eyed): Wow. Tell me about it.

For the next 10 minutes, as the twinkling lights of the Vegas Strip grew ever closer, the Expert managed to convince his impressionable listener to quit playing a game, blackjack, that averages less than .5% advantage for the house (with perfect play) to one, Caribbean Stud poker, in which the house advantage is a stern 5.3%. The Student could now look forward to spending her weekend playing a game with at least 10 times *worse* odds than her usual choice.

Fact is, most gamblers know the games they like, but they don't know how much these games are likely to cost them in the long run. Indeed, few casino visitors realize that not all the games are created equal, that some bets are truly better—or worse—than others. Believe it or not, some of the best bets actually work in the *player's* favor; these deserve to be inducted into the casino bettor's Hall of Fame. The worst bets are so larcenous they deserve inclusion in the Hall of Shame.

THE HALL OF FAME
Top Five Best Bets in the Casino

#5) Craps, "Line Bet": -1.4%

Of all the myriad—and sometimes inscrutable—options on the dice layout, betting on "the line" is the most basic wager. And easily one of the best deals. Players gamble on whether the "shooter" (the player rolling the dice) will "make his number" (roll a predetermined number) or throw a losing 7. Conversely, you can bet that the shooter won't make his number. This option is called "don't pass." Both line bets, the pass and don't pass, are paid at even money: Bet $10, win $10.

If you bet the shooter will pass, and his very first roll of the dice (the "come-out" roll) is a 7 or 11, you win. (After the first roll, if a point has been established, any 7 is a loser.) If the dice come up 2, 3, or 12, you lose. The casino gains its small advantage by taking money from "pass" players on the 12 and not paying off the "don't pass" players. Still, when you make a line bet, with its -1.4% expectation, in the long run you will lose only $14 for every $1,000 you gamble.

#4) Baccarat, "Bank Bet": -1.15%

If you enjoy the challenge of calling heads or tails on a coin flip, baccarat is for you. Though the casinos toil mightily to imbue the game with enough faux glamour—crystal chandeliers, tuxedo-clad dealers, free-flowing champagne—to make even the grungiest gambler believe he's the living incarnation of James Bond, the game requires absolutely no decision-making other than picking heads or tails. Or in this case, "player" or "bank." (There's a third bet, "tie"—but more on that nefarious option later.)

Two hands of cards are dealt. The one with a point total closest to 9 wins. Because of some arcane rules involving when an extra card will be drawn, the bank hand has a slight advantage over the player. Alas, if you bet on the bank, you must pay a 5% commission on your winnings. Thus the

121

casino's small edge.

Incidentally, the player bet, with an expectation of –1.37%, slightly less attractive than bank, still qualifies for the casino bettor's Hall of Fame.

#3) Blackjack, Basic Strategy: -.5% to 0%

One of the most popular games in the casino also happens to be one of the best values—if you play basic strategy. That's a big "if." Gamblers who make their "hit" or "stand" decisions on hunches, emotions, or some far-fetched theory their cousin Jed told them will see their bankrolls shrink faster than a raisin in the sun. Those who master basic strategy will enjoy one of the fairest gambles in the casino. Furthermore, if you can find a single-deck game with favorable rules—dealer stands on soft 17, etc.—the casino edge can be reduced to 0%. If you learn a simple card-counting system, blackjack can even become a positive-expectation gamble: In many cases you have the advantage.

Basic strategy is a set of easily memorized playing decisions based on the dealer's up-card and the player's total: Hit your 16 vs. the dealer's 7, stand on 13 vs. the dealer's 6, double down on your pair of 5s vs. the dealer's 8, and so forth. (Reliable basic strategy tables can be found in almost any blackjack book written after 1970.) Each play in the basic strategy matrix has been tested with billions of computer-simulated hands. Follow the guidelines and you'll always be making the unequivocal *best* decision. You will be playing perfectly. And enjoying a nearly break-even game.

#2) Craps, Maximum Odds: -.018% to -.002%

After you've made your line bet—#5 in the Hall of Fame—you can "back up" your initial wager with a "behind-the-line" bet, called "odds." This secondary bet is paid at true odds; the casino has *no* advantage on this wager. Many casinos let gamblers bet only twice the amount of their line bet, or "double" odds. More liberal casinos allow odds bets of 10 times (10x) the initial wager ($10 on the line and $100 behind; a .018% house advantage). And some periodically offer 100x odds, which, if you have a large enough bankroll to fade the fluctuations, is a terrific deal. In this case, you're betting $100 at true odds, with no house edge, and $1 at a 1.4% disadvantage. The cumulative effect is a bet that in the long run loses only two pennies for every $1,000 you wager.

"If everybody who played dice took the full odds," Jack Binion, president of Binion's Horseshoe in downtown Las Vegas, has said, "we couldn't pay our light bill."

#1) Video Poker, Selected Machines: +100.7%

With perfect play, certain video poker machines return more than $1 for every dollar you wager. That makes them the rarest beast in the casino jungle: a "positive-expectation" bet.

Unlike slot machines, the amount of jackpots a video poker machine pays out cannot be manipulated by the casino; the house can't cook the results. In the long run, every video poker machine will produce the "correct" number of royal flushes, full houses, and so on that the odds say it should. The only way for the house to get an edge, therefore, is to tweak the payout schedule, returning, for example, five coins on a flush instead of the six that the better machines pay. Savvy gamblers who find "full-pay" machines can, in the long run, beat the house.

There are dozens of different video poker machines, most of which operate with a casino advantage of anywhere between .3% and 8%. Several types give the player the advantage: deuces wild (100.7% return) and double bonus poker (100.17% return).

The casinos can afford to sprinkle these machines throughout their floors since most gamblers don't play well enough to beat them, even with the built-in edge. To learn expert strategy for beatable forms of video poker, you can consult any number of guidebooks, including *Bob Dancer's*

Video Poker Reports.

To find a machine you can beat, you need to examine the pay tables carefully. A "classic" deuces wild machine pays as follows: 25 coins for a wild royal flush; 15 for 5-of-a-kind; 9 for a straight flush; and 5 for 4-of-a-kind. Double bonus machines that give an edge to the player are known as 10/7 machines: 10 coins for a full house, 7 for a flush. Play these babies strictly according to the proper strategy in combination with a slot club rebate, and ultimately the casino will be paying you for the pleasure of your company.

THE HALL OF SHAME
Top Five Worst Bets in the Casino

Not surprisingly, action-hungry gamblers can find far more bad bets in a casino than good ones. That's how these joints can afford to offer prime rib dinners for $4.95. Even something as seemingly innocuous as the insurance bet at blackjack (-14.3%) is a horrible play. Remember this general caveat: Any game that offers a large, sometimes life-changing, jackpot is almost without exception a terrible bet. Though not quite as kleptomaniacal as state lotteries, which often operate at a *50% house advantage,* most casino games (other than video poker) that have an ever-climbing meter attached to them, should be avoided. As the savvy *Las Vegas Advisor* newsletter reported not long ago, some of the public's favorite "linked progressive" slot machines (where money from around a state is pooled into a huge jackpot) are among the worst bets in the casino. But even those aren't as bad as our Top Five thieves.

#5) Baccarat, "Tie Bet": -14.4%
The tuxedo-clad dealers who shill for the tie bet—"Anyone betting a tie? Tie bet, anyone? Place your tie bet!"—are not paid a commission by the house. They ought to be. This

one is a huge moneymaker for the casino.

You'll often see big baccarat players filling out and studying charts, trying to discern a pattern in the past results, forgetting, of course, that these results have no bearing on the future. You can almost see the epiphany flashing across their minds: *"My god, there hasn't been a tie for twelve hands! I should bet the tie."* Well, actually they shouldn't. Ever. This bet is 11 times worse than wagering on player or bank.

#4) Craps, "Any 7": -16.7%

As good as the line and odds bets are, that's how rotten the "proposition" bets are on a dice table. You'll find an array of these come-ons in the middle of the table. The worst of these one-roll wagers is the "any 7," in which a gambler bets that the very next roll of the bones will produce a total of 7.

Anyone with a grade-school aptitude for math should see the folly of this bet, which pays only 5-for-1 when the true odds are 6-for-1. But Gambling Fever tends to affect eyesight as well.

#3) The Big Wheel, Any Bet: -19.1% (average edge)

The big wheel, or "big six" as it's often called, looks like a salvage job from a long-shuttered carnival: *"Spin the wheel; win a prize!"* Casinos frequently employ their peppiest "people persons" at the big wheel, where, management hopes, ignorant gamblers will get caught up in the simulated carnival atmosphere.

There's nothing worth gambling on here. If you see anyone parked in front of this spinning money drain, you can be sure he's either very drunk or very stupid. The "best" bet, on the $1 spot, gives the casino an 11.1% advantage. The worst, on one of two jokers that pays 40-to-1, skims 24%. Everything in between is just as bad, producing an average edge for the house approaching a usurious 20%.

#2) Keno: -28%

This number may be slightly generous. Some keno games give the casino an advantage of well over 30%!

The house picks 20 numbered balls out of a pool of 80. Players attempt to match as few as one of the numbers or as many as all 20, depending on how they play. In every configuration of the game—pick five, 20-spot special, and so on—the casinos skew the payouts so wickedly that you'd think the wretchedness of the game would be painfully obvious. You'd be mistaken.

Just remember this the next time the fellow next to you on the plane boasts of his latest keno triumph: Anyone who claims to have a system for beating keno is either sadly mistaken or a pathological liar.

#1) Caribbean Stud Poker, "Bonus Side Bet": -47%

It's just a dollar. One measly extra dollar, and—who knows?—it could make you rich.

That's what the casinos hope gamblers are thinking when they play Caribbean Stud: "If I bet the extra dollar and the dealer gives me a royal flush, I'll win fifty or a hundred thousand, or maybe a couple million. If I don't bet it, I can't win the big bonus."

Here are the facts. You'll receive a five-card royal flush about once every 648,000 hands. At Caribbean Stud tables, generous casinos will pay you upward of $100,000 for this once-in-a-lifetime occurrence. Stingy ones pay as little as $25,000.

Think of it this way: Every time you see someone plunk down a dollar on this bonus side bet, he is, in effect, asking for change. But instead of getting back four quarters, he happily accepts 53¢. That, it seems, is the price one pays to cure a bad case of Gambling Fever.

14

Taking Advantage

"Let me show you something," Steve Forte says. "Go ahead, shuffle the cards."

We're sitting on opposite sides of a marble coffee table, in a hotel room 30 stories above the Strip. I break open the plastic-wrap seal on a fresh pack of Bee playing cards, the brand used at hundreds of casinos around the world.

"Here's what I want you to do," Forte says. "Give them a good riffle, then cut. Then riffle again. Then cut. Then a final riffle and cut."

I do as directed. "Great. Now, Mike, you've basically executed the identical shuffle used in some of the biggest casinos in Las Vegas, the ones that take the largest bets in the world. You would think they'd go to great lengths to thoroughly mix their cards, to achieve true randomness, right?"

I nod. "Of course."

"Deal me four hands of twenty-one," Forte says, pointing to the coffee table. "I'll bet an imaginary twenty-five dollars a hand. Deal yourself a hand, too. And don't let me see your hole card. You're the house."

We play out the first four hands. Forte "loses" three of them to my 19. "Good. This worked out really well," he says, smiling. "It's not always this easy."

"What do you mean?" I ask.

"Well, it just so happens that the next card off the deck, if I'm not mistaken, will be the ace of spades. Then, six cards later, we'll see the ace of hearts. So I'll give you some decent play on those spots, like five hundred a hand."

I deal out the cards. Forte's aces appear exactly as predicted. He seems as unsurprised as I am flabbergasted. "Getting an ace as your first card in twenty-one gives you fifty percent advantage over the house," he explains. "It doesn't get much stronger than that."

Forte hasn't touched the cards. He allowed me to shuffle and cut the deck, and I'm certain the cards aren't marked. I feel like a child at his first magic show. "How did you do that?"

"Did you look at your hole card, Mike?"

"No, should I?"

"Nah, don't bother," he says, smiling. "It's the seven of hearts."

* * *

Steve Forte is the president of International Gaming Specialists, a consulting firm that works with casinos worldwide on "game protection," teaching them how to defend their tables from cheaters, scam artists, and surprisingly, themselves. Because of inadequate procedures, exploitable equipment, or lax supervision, many casinos leave themselves exposed to what's known in the industry as "advantage players," exploiters who use all available information and any legitimate strategy to gain an edge. These players annually beat the casinos out of millions.

Formerly one of the world's most successful professional gamblers, Forte is intimately familiar with every advantage play to hit the casinos in the last 10 years. He's widely credited with conceiving many of them.

"In the last decade, advantage players have had more effect on the gambling industry than cheaters ever had," Forte says. "Casinos regularly overhaul their game procedures because advantage players discover profitable weaknesses." The emergence of card counters, for example, forced casinos to deal only two-thirds or three-quarters of a deck, instead of down to the bottom as they used to. But the vast majority of people who go to casinos have no idea these powerful advantage techniques exist. The average "square John" (sucker) and the skilled advantage player look like they're playing the same game. The only difference is the advantage player wins.

Some of the advantage plays Forte employed in his former career were known to a few hundred people in the world; some were known by only a few dozen. I've asked Forte to share some of these powerful techniques, most of which have never before been revealed in the mainstream press.

He warns me that advantage plays are not merely "tricks," infallible gimmicks that will turn losers into winners. These methods take hours of practice, require significant mental agility, and often prove too difficult for the casual gambler. Applied incorrectly, some advantage techniques will cost players more money than if they simply tried to get lucky.

Applied correctly, they can destroy the casino's edge.

Blackjack and Baccarat

Forte has me shuffle the cards again and deal out several hands of blackjack. With seemingly extrasensory precision he correctly predicts where the aces will fall, which suit will appear first, and the value of my hole card.

"It's called 'shuffle tracking,'" he says.

Initially mentioned around the turn of the century in an obscure magic book by Charles Jordan and C.O. Williams, shuffle tracking, or sequence tracking, is an advantage technique Steve Forte first employed in the mid-'80s. To create true randomness, a deck of 52 cards needs to be shuffled at least seven times. But the more casinos shuffle, the more money they "lose," because their profits are a function of how many hands they get out per hour. (The more hands they deal to suckers, the more money they win.) So virtually all the casinos in America shuffle their decks an average of only three times. Sequence tracking exploits the vulnerability created by inadequate shuffling.

When shuffled purely, cards will "move" to an easily predicted spot in the deck. If, for example, the ace of spades immediately follows the three of diamonds in the deck, after one riffle the ace will be the second card away from the trey; another riffle will leave it four cards down; and a third will leave it eight cards from its original position. (Turn two touching cards face up, shuffle the deck, and see for yourself.) By memorizing three-card sequences—usually two "key cards" preceding or surrounding the "target card" (an ace)—the accomplished sequence tracker can collect enough data to follow the progress of desired cards through the casino's not-at-all-random mixing procedure.

At my request, Forte demonstrates the practicality of continuous tracking: As he correctly predicts where the aces will fall on the first deal, he also memorizes sequences to be applied on the next deal. Sure enough, five deals in a row provide him with a steady stream of aces on his imaginary big-money bets.

I ask Forte if sequence tracking works in multi-deck games, including baccarat.

"Absolutely," he says.

In fact, the "lace" shuffle most casinos use in their high-limit baccarat pits—where the dealer often exposes five- and six-card clumps to the player nearest him—creates memorizable "slugs" (distinct sequences), making the game particularly vulnerable to advantage players.

Not long ago, a series of enlightening articles in the periodical *Blackjack Forum*, a quarterly aimed at sophisticated players, included detailed instructions on how to create a schematic of all known casino blackjack shuffles.

"Before sequence tracking, advantage players do research," Forte reports. "Dealer selection is crucial. You want to find a dealer who breaks the cards evenly and shuffles correctly, just like they're taught in dealer school. Female dealers, especially ones with small, delicate hands are often the best targets."

While staking out a casino for trackable dealers, advantage players look for *hole-card plays,* blackjack dealers inadvertently exposing their hole cards to the players. The advantage is obvious: When you know the dealer is "stiff" (holding 12-16) and prone to bust, you can waver from basic strategy and stand on bad hands you would otherwise hit.

"You'd be surprised how many dealers give up their hole card," Forte reveals. "At one point, with some research, I had a journal of three-hundred Las Vegas dealers susceptible to hole-card play. Walk around any casino in America and look carefully: The serious advantage player can still find them." (In 10 minutes of strolling through one of the most famous casinos on the Vegas Strip, Forte finds me three.)

Some dealers have distinct *tells,* the subconscious body language commonly associated with poker, the subtle mannerisms and gestures that frequently expose the value of a hand. Until 1986, nearly 100% of the blackjack dealers in Nevada "peeked" at their hole card if they had an ace or a ten-value card up. (They were looking for naturals, instant winners for the house.) Then Steve Forte published a booklet called *Read the Dealer,* which taught advantage players how to discern the dealer's hole card through non-verbal signals. Thanks to Forte's powerful treatise—a book that helped teams of "tell players" win fortunes—dealers at only about 15% of the casinos in America currently peek. Many of these dealers unwittingly employ a vocabulary of physical or verbal signs that the astute player can use to his advantage.

Though reading dealer tells is a rich and complex science that requires some practice, here are a couple of basic guidelines the pros search for: A dealer who is rooting for the players to win will usually lean away from the table when he has a bad hand and lean into it when he's pat. And in a single- or double-deck game when a dealer is pat, he'll usually keep his non-deck hand far from his body; when he has a stiff, the non-deck hand will wander inward, away from the players, as if to say, "You're fine. Let me take the hit."

Another way to exploit dealer-furnished information is *playing the warps.* For this technique, advantage players look for male dealers, particularly big overpowering types who handle the cards aggressively. When this kind of dealer looks under his tens or aces to check for blackjacks, he's prone to put a readable warp into the cards. At a casino where the dealers peek under all aces and ten-value cards, it doesn't take long for the deck to become "set up": All the little cards get bent one way (convex) and all the premium cards get bent the other way (concave).

It's true. Playing in a small Egyptian casino several years ago, I encountered an old deck so hopelessly buckled, it was like playing with the cards face up. In such a deck the big cards create discernible bows, distinct "breaths" between cards. I didn't know back then how to exploit this information. Astute players can consistently cut themselves an ace or ten after the shuffle—a spectacular 20% average advantage.

One caveat: When the dealer warps the deck, it's an advantage play; when *you* warp the deck, it's against the law. Resist the urge to assist.

"I'll tell you one more advantage technique," Forte says conspiratorially. "Playing with a marked deck."

"But that's cheating," I say.

"Not if the person marking the deck is the card manufacturer!" Forte says, grinning.

He has me pitch him several hands of 21. Then he asks for the deck. "Here, Mike," Forte says, dealing two piles of cards, "you take those and I'll take these." I turn over my pile of cards: They're all little ones. Forte turns over his: He's got all the aces and faces.

"We call that 'playing the turn.'"

The vast majority of decks, he explains, including the Bee variety we're experimenting with, are cut slightly off-center. At first glance, the backs all look the same, but if you examine the edges carefully, the small "triangles" around the sides vary dramatically (to the trained eye) in size.

"As he receives his cards, the advantage player simply turns the cards to the desired alignment. Eventually, after a few deals, he's got the deck 'marked.' All the little cards have the little triangles on top; all the big ones have big triangles on top." Playing the turn provides hole-card information and top-of-the-deck values—and it's perfectly legal.

Craps

Forte and I go downstairs to the casino—one of the most famous gambling halls in the world. I point to a crap table.

"Unbeatable, right?" I ask.

"Wrong," Forte says matter-of-factly. "There's a lot of controversy surrounding this game. Has a player cheated by controlling his shot? According to the laws of physics, it's impossible to dictate how to throw the dice."

"You're saying advantage players can control the outcome of the dice roll?" I'm incredulous.

"Absolutely. Only a few people can do it, but yes, there are several methods. 'Walking the die,' where one die wobbles around its axis but never changes position; 'spin shots,' where the shooter 'slides' the dice down the felt; 'puck' or 'wall shots,' where the shooter kills a number off the disc they use to mark the point—rule out nothing."

Several weeks later, demonstrating for a group of students at the William F. Harrah Institute of Casino Entertainment, Forte blithely rolls double sixes three times in a row, a 43,000-1 proposition. Watching from two feet away, I am no longer incredulous.

Slots and Video Poker

We pass a bank of video poker machines. "Those," Forte

says, pointing to a row of $1 9/6 jacks or better machines, "cannot be beaten. But *those*," he says, gesturing to a bank of $1 8/5 units with a progressive jackpot meter at $2,700, "definitely are beatable. Many knowledgeable gamblers play video poker for a living. You have to know which machines to play and the correct strategy for playing them. For instance, in most home poker games, if you were dealt ace-jack [of different suits] along with seven-five-trey, you would keep the ace, or maybe the ace-jack. Here, the correct play is to keep only the jack."

Then we pass a bank of slot machines. I shoot Forte a look that says, "Don't tell me there's an advantage technique for slots!"

"No, unfortunately, today's slot machines work on a micro-chip," he says. "You can't beat them. But up until the early eighties, when they still used electro-mechanical machines, you could definitely win at slots using what we called 'rythming,' timing the machine's so-called variator. The machines definitely did not produce true randomness. You might find these old machines, like Bally's Widebody Fruit, in some foreign casinos, but not here," Forte says, somewhat wistfully.

"But I'll show you one old game that's still vulnerable to advantage play."

Roulette

We stop at a roulette wheel. "Albert Einstein once said you couldn't win at roulette unless you were stealing chips." Forte shrugs. "I guess even geniuses make mistakes."

Forte instructs me to watch where the ball falls off the track and into the dish of spinning numbers. It loses its momentum and dives down at the "10 o'clock" position. On the next spin it does it again. And again. And again. Thirteen times in a row. "There's no such thing as a perfect wheel," Forte says. "They're basically a piece of furniture. They take abuse, they get dirty, they get worn down. They produce biased results." Using a technique called *visual pre-*

diction, advantage players exploit the wheel's imperfections.

Outlined in an obscure book by Lawrence Scott called *Beating the Wheel,* the visual prediction method is built on an immutable law of physics: Regardless of how fast the ball is spun by the dealer, it must necessarily *end* at the same speed. Advantage players beat the wheel from the "back" of the spin, not the front. They play the last four or five revolutions of the ball. After finding a wheel with a clear bias—Forte says there's probably at least one in every major casino in America—they clock the speed of the rotor (the spinning dish of numbers), looking for one that takes between two and three seconds per revolution. (This is surprisingly easy to time in your head, even without a watch with a second hand.) By correlating the speed of the rotor with the ball's predictable "drop point," the advantage player can gauge which number will be sitting directly under the ball when it dives into the dish. Even taking into account the volatility of the ball's bounce, when betting late enough in the spin, advantage players can essentially narrow the list of probable numbers from 38 to 19, obliterating the house's normal 5% edge.

In the course of Forte's explanation of visual prediction, the ball has fallen off the same spot on the wheel 25 out of 27 times.

At a nearby high-limit blackjack table, he's detected the dealer's hole card four of the last five hands.

And at the crap table behind us, they're looking for a new shooter.

I've promised Steve Forte lunch. But I'd rather buy him a rack of chips.

Sports Betting

Sports
Betting

15

The Line Maker

When the San Francisco 49ers defeated the San Diego Chargers, 49-26, in the 1995 Super Bowl, most people viewing the game were less concerned about which team would take home the Lombardi Trophy than about who would beat the point spread. Whether wagering $5 in the office pool, betting the mortgage payment with an illegal bookie, or making a recreational gamble at one of Nevada's 100-plus licensed sports books, a vast majority of the Super Bowl audience had money riding on the game's outcome—including me and, no doubt, many of you. Some experts estimate $5 billion is bet on Super Bowl Sunday, most of it illegally.

That the majority of us had either San Diego plus 19 points or San Francisco minus 19 was the work of Michael Roxborough. "Roxy," as he likes to be called, is the man who sets the Las Vegas line, which, in turn, becomes America's line, and the world's line. When you call your bookie in Milwaukee to find out how many points the Bucks are giving to the Clippers, the number you'll hear was gleaned indirectly from Roxy. When Al Michaels and Dan Dierdorf slyly joke about the over/under total on Monday Night Football ("If the Lions kick this field goal, the game will truly be *over,* in more ways than one!"), the number they're referring to came from Roxy. And when you saunter into the sports book at a Vegas casino and see a phalanx of propositions on football, baseball, basketball, hockey, boxing, NASCAR and Indy racing, the World Cup, tennis, even PGA golf, the one bet you can be reasonably sure of is that Roxy Roxborough is the guy who came up with the odds.

At first glance you'd probably assume Roxy Roxborough was anything but the king of linemakers. If you were to mistakenly wander into his suite in an office park across from Las Vegas' McCarran airport, you might think Roxy Roxborough more apt to prepare your taxes than declare the Knicks a 6-to-1 dog to win the NBA Championship. His buttoned-down mien is no accident. "We run this business as a corporation, objectively. Over two billion dollars were bet in Nevada sports books this year. We can't afford to get involved emotionally."

His company, Las Vegas Sports Consultants, employs a staff of analysts and clerks who, with the aid of computers, newswires, and video monitors, determine the relative power of every team and every player in America that someone might conceivably want to bet on. Then they make "the line," a numerical expression of probability. Contrary to a popular misconception, Roxy and his people do not have inside information, nor are they in the business of predicting the final outcome of a sporting contest. An oddsmaker's job is to generate action. Generally, the larger the bookmaker's handle, the more profit.

"Oddsmaking is a little art and a little science," Roxy says, watching the Chargers make a third-quarter drive against the heavily favored Steelers in the 1995 AFC Championship game. "Sports are so well-covered these days, especially the NFL, that we have virtually the same amount of information as the sharp gambler. Having the information is not difficult; it's the interpretation of that information that makes a difference."

He pumps his fist as the Chargers score a go-ahead touchdown. "You'll probably never see me this excited about a game," he says dispassionately. "In fact, I generally try not to watch. But everybody in the world is on Pittsburgh, and we really need San Diego. It's by far the biggest game of the year for us."

By "us," Roxy means the casinos. The Nevada sports books are his clients, paying him between $1,500 and $2,800 a month for odds, updates, and reports; they are who he roots for. (His odds also appear in syndication in more than 100 newspapers.) Though many of Roxy's odds produce "two-way action," where the betting is balanced on both sides, some, by design, do not. In those cases, such as the AFC Championship game, the bookmakers badly need one team. "The money is pretty balanced on the NFC game," Roxy says, glancing at one of the many computer terminals that line his office. "But the AFC game will be a multi-million-dollar decision."

Despite the prodigious sums at stake, Roxy claims to hate watching the games. "In the six hours it takes to watch two football games, I can analyze fifty teams. At this point in my life, all the teams, all the players, are simply numbers." He rubs his chin pensively. "The irony is ninety-five percent of the public bet for entertainment, for the rush of adrenalin you get in the last two minutes, when your money is on the line. Like everyone else, I started out as a sports fan. Now I'd rather listen to ocean music."

Given his background, the line against Roxy one day becoming the heir to Bob "The Man" Martin, Las Vegas' previous Arbiter of the Odds, must have been about 100 million-to-1. After a respectable Vancouver, B.C., childhood, a stint managing a fast-food restaurant, and a few semesters at American University, where he majored in betting the ponies, Roxy settled in Las Vegas in 1976. "I came to Vegas to be a professional gambler, so I wouldn't have to hold a conventional job. But I ended up working sixty hours a week at gambling to escape working forty hours a week."

He was particularly successful at betting baseball totals, charting wind and atmospheric conditions at the ballparks. "Today, no bookmaker would think of posting odds without getting a weather forecast. Back then, believe it or not, no one ever checked." He was so proficient that the sports book at the Club Cal-Neva in Reno asked him to set its baseball totals. Soon Roxy was making the line on all sports across the board. With only a single customer, he founded Las Vegas Sports Consultants in 1982, working from his kitchen table. Assignments at other northern Nevada casinos followed, and in 1983 Roxy landed the high-profile job of setting the "opening line" for the Stardust. "I had to decide then if I wanted to be a professional gambler or a professional oddsmaker. I felt doing both would be a conflict of interest. I gave up sports betting and became an oddsmaker."

"I'd be happy if he retired," says Lem Banker, a well-known Vegas sports bettor with a 36-year reputation. "He's a very smart fellow, a very astute handicapper, and he makes a tough line."

According to Gary Olshan, chief analyst at *The Gold Sheet*, a handicapping newsletter for sophisticated gamblers, "Everyone who bets sports has great respect for Roxy. He's got a difficult job and he does it superbly. The lines have gotten a lot tougher since he took over."

Though Roxy no longer bets on the games—indeed, he owns a 10% stake in a Nevada bookmaking operation called Leroy's—he didn't forsake his "hobby" of betting on horseracing. He's characteristically modest about his equine accomplishments, but Roxy is one of only three voting members of the National Turf Writer's Association in Nevada, contributes odds on the Triple Crown and Breeders' Cup races to the *Daily Racing Form*, and has owned several thoroughbreds. He's visited 65 tracks in seven countries, making a few wagers here and there. In 1992, for example, he hit the Pick 9 at Santa Anita, winning $108,000. Naturally, his office is decorated with signed racing programs and horse memorabilia.

Also hanging on the wall is a plastic bag containing a nylon rope. It says, "For: A middle on Super Bowl."

If, indeed, the sports books were to get "middled" on the Super Bowl (beaten by bettors on *both* sides of the ac-

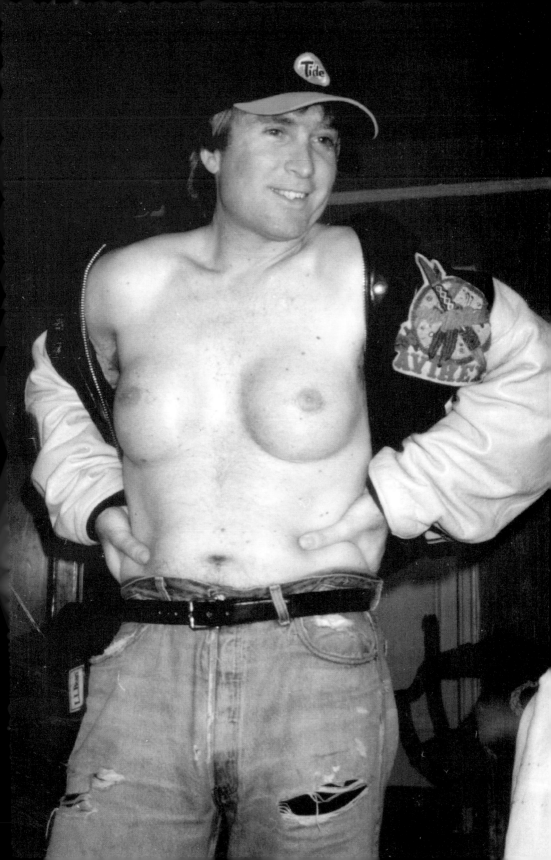

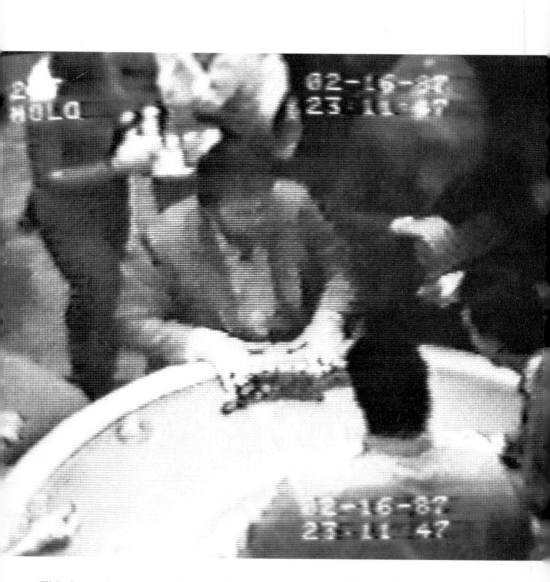

This frame from a surveillance video captures the Cold-Deck Crew's "Big Player" in action. The chips on the layout amount to roughly $90,000.

previous page: Brian Zembic—the man with the $100,000 breasts.

David James used a nerdy high-school-reunion photo to sell his sports picks—then had his four-year-old son make the selections.

Michael "Roxy" Roxborough makes the "Las Vegas line," used by bookies—legal and illegal—throughout the world. (Larry Grossman)

Andy Beyer, the world's premier horse handicapper, gets emotionally involved in a race at Pimlico. (Dennis Brack)

right: During a few magic months in Las Vegas, Archie Karas turned a borrowed stake of $10,000 into $17 million. (courtesy of Binion's Horseshoe)

Young lions Phil Hellmuth Jr. (top)
and Huck Seed (bottom) were both
World Series of Poker Champions
before the age of 30.
(Larry Grossman)

left: They called him the "Grand
Old Man" of poker. At one time,
all poker waters flowed through
Johnny Moss. (Larry Grossman)

Michael Jordan, Bill Gates, and George Bush all keep lockers at Shadow Creek, where only the highest of rollers play the $1,000-per-round golf course. (courtesy of Mirage Resorts, Inc.)

tion because of an inaccurate line that had to be moved several points), more than a few people in Roxy's business might be mildly suicidal. But the fact is, in the past 20 Super Bowls, the line has been involved only thrice in the wagering decision. In 1997, the Packers won by 14, the exact point spread, over New England. In 1988 the 49ers won, but failed to cover. And in 1978 the Steelers beat the Cowboys 35-31. Because of a line that moved from -2$\frac{1}{2}$ to -4$\frac{1}{2}$, many books suffered the dreaded middle. The vast majority of times, though, to cash a winning ticket on the Super Bowl, bettors have had to pick only the game's victor independent of the point spread. According to that line of reasoning, the 1995 Super Bowl was an easy decision: Take San Francisco and lay the points, no matter how high the line.

Roxy, of course, is aware of such trends. Though most of the odds he posts are aimed at the so-called "smart money," the sophisticates who bet sports for a living, the Super Bowl line is aimed at the masses, the casual gamblers. Before the 1995 NFC Championship game between San Francisco and Dallas begins, Roxy posts two numbers on a large bulletin board: SF 16 and D 13$\frac{1}{2}$. "These are my tentative numbers against San Diego," he announces. "Let's see how the game goes." After San Francisco takes a commanding first-quarter lead, Roxy changes the "SF" number to 16$\frac{1}{2}$. "I don't know," he says, thinking out loud, "it just doesn't look right." But before he and his associates can refine the Super Bowl odds, Roxy must issue the line for half-time betting on this game. Based on the Niners' first-half domination, Emmit Smith's hamstring troubles, and Jerry Rice's improbable last-second score, Roxy makes San Francisco a -140 favorite (bet $140 to win $100) to "win" the second half. As the first-half game clock expires, an employee enters Roxy's odds on a computer; instantaneously, his line is posted all over Nevada, Mexico, England, and everywhere else Las Vegas Sports Consultants has clients.

Within seconds, thanks to LVSC's on-line update system, Roxy learns the betting public's response to his line:

Big money is pouring in—all on the Cowboys. Like a currency trader unloading millions of pesos, Roxy quickly "trades" the number downward. "Minus one-thirty," he says, staring at a computer screen, trying to discern if the move has attracted any money on the San Francisco side. "Go to one-twenty," he orders. Seconds later he shakes his head incredulously and says, "Okay, make it even." Remarkably, the money is *still* pouring in on the Cowboys. Apparently the bettors think Dallas will rally in the second half and make the game close. *"Cowboys* minus one-thirty," Roxy says, smiling sheepishly.

Finally, the action stabilizes. "I guess we were on the wrong side of that one," Roxy says. "It happens." The phone rings. The sports book manager of a major Strip property wants to know, "Who made that line? Your girlfriend?"

"We botched that one," Roxy says to his client, matter-of-factly. "Hey, get yourself another Ouija board."

As soon as the second half starts, Roxy retreats to his office to begin formulating proposition bets for the Super Bowl. "The closer the game is to a pick 'em [a 50/50 matchup] the more betting you'll see. With a point spread as big as we'll be forced to make for San Diego-San Francisco, or even San Diego-Dallas, we'll need a lot more props to generate action." Poring over statistics and computer analyses, Roxy issues odds on dozens of exotic wagers: "most sacks," "total yards," "first scorer," etc. (According to one professional bettor, the price for a safety occurring—12-to-1—was a decent value. It didn't happen. Jerry Rice being the first to score a touchdown—3-to-1—did.)

Later, when it becomes clear the Niners have handily vanquished the Cowboys (and covered the 7-point spread and won the second half), Roxy positions himself between two key staffers, his odds manager, Scott Kaminsky, and one of his chief oddsmakers, Cesar Robaina, and says, "Okay, let's get to work." He erases the 16 1/2 next on the board and writes "17."

"I'm thinking seventeen and fifty-one [the total number of points scored], though I'm also inclined to go a little higher," Roxy says.

"There's no defense that can stop San Francisco," Kaminsky says. "I'm leaning toward eighteen or even nineteen. Total domination."

"San Diego needs turnovers. That's the only way they'll stay in the game," Robaina comments.

"So you like eighteen?" Roxy asks.

"I think seventeen and a half is good," Robaina replies.

Roxy looks at a computer printout of the teams' respective power ratings. He shakes his head. "Look, the computer makes no difference right now. We need to find a number that will make someone bet on San Diego. We know San Diego won't win. But we need to start with a number that will generate some action. We've got to put up a number that will make everyone who wants to bet on San Francisco think twice. 'Do I really want to lay that many points?' I think seventeen and a half is a good place to start. Seventeen and a half and fifty-two. That seems right."

"San Francisco has really become America's team. They've demolished everybody they've faced in big games. Of course, we can always move it up," Kaminsky agrees.

"Okay," Roxy announces. "Seventeen and a half and fifty-two." In less than two minutes he's decided the opening line for a game that will attract billions of dollars in wagers. "Put it on the system," he says.

Seconds later, every phone in the office starts ringing. Newspapers from all around Nevada, the rest of America, and even Canada want to hear Roxy's reasoning. "It's simple," he tells them. "We've seen throughout the season that nobody will bet San Diego. We want to give them a reason to change that."

Caesars Palace is the first major Las Vegas casino to release a Super Bowl line: Tweaking Roxy's number slightly, they open at 18 and 52. Four other of Roxy's major Strip clients mull the point spread for five minutes before posting the 17 1/2 and 52 figures. The MGM Grand opens at 17 and immediately books several sizable bets on the 49ers. Kaminsky reports the news to Roxy. "Go to eighteen," he orders. By early evening, most Vegas sports books are dealing San Francisco at minus 18 1/2. By the next day it's 19, and the total has moved up to 53 1/2. Though one Vegas casino briefly posts 20 for a few hours as a publicity stunt, in the days preceding the big game the number settles in the 18 1/2 and 19 range.

"I think we've done a good job," Roxy says a few days before Super Bowl Sunday. "We seem to have found a number that's bringing in some action on San Diego. Of course, we won't know where this is going until the Friday before the game. That's when the big money starts coming in."

Where would his money be if he were betting?

"I think a lot of wiseguys will be sitting this one out. But if I had to make a pick, I'd be taking the Chargers and the points. That's where the value is—and that's where you'll probably see the wiseguys betting."

A few days after San Francisco whipped San Diego, 49-26 (which, to Roxy's surprise, attracted a record handle, including a single $2.4 million wager at the Mirage), America's linemaker is circumspect. "We clearly did a good job. The consensus line never moved more than two points. We ended up winning the straight bets, the props, the half-time bets, and the futures. But we got beat on the parlays— the 'favorite' and 'over' parlay. [Bettors who picked both the 49ers and more than 52 points total earned 13-to-5 on their wagers.] Of the four scenarios, only one—favorite and over—beats us. And that's the one that came in."

He shrugs. "San Diego scores on their last drive, we go from a medium loser to a big winner." Roxy smiles. "That's why they call it gambling."

16

Living by the Book

From the outside, the decrepit building in one of New York City's worst neighborhoods looks like every other decrepit building on the block. A bum, smashed on cheap hooch, lies in a heap at the foot of the stairs. Skinny teenagers with desperate eyes roam the sidewalks like hungry coyotes prowling for a crippled rodent. And small-time crack peddlers, a malt liquor in one hand and a plastic bag of potent pebbles in the other, openly ply their trade on the street corner, oblivious to the police sirens that never seem to stop wailing.

It is not a glamorous spot, this block.

But inside this particular tenement, in a rented apartment nearly as slovenly as the surroundings, where you might otherwise expect a low-rent prostitute to set up shop, business is booming.

Hidden by the facade of squalor, several Ivy League-educated entrepreneurs answer the phones, receiving frantic calls from around America. Like stock traders in the throes of a bull market, they bark out strings of numbers: "minus one-twenty," "plus three and a half," "over thirty-seven." Simultaneously scribbling orders on pre-printed "tickets" and eavesdropping on their colleagues' transactions, each member of this crew of former scholars has the numerical talent and mental nimbleness of a commodities trader swapping Krugerrands for pesetas. They're quick-witted, these boys. In every transaction, they seek a minuscule edge, the nearly invisible spread that separates winners from losers. Where their clients see only a chance for the fleeting frisson of action, they see an opportunity for financial well-being.

These furtive laborers are rich. And unlike most fellows their age, they got that way without having to master the art of obsequiousness, toadying to a powerful boss whom they neither like nor respect. Though they surely would have made successful bankers or lawyers or arbitrageurs, these young men shunned the suit-and-tie life in favor of becoming bookies.

* * *

Who among us has not laid the points on a Monday Night Football game? Who hasn't bet on a heavyweight title fight? The World Series, the Super Bowl, March Madness? Tens of millions bet on sports, and, because most of us don't live in Nevada, the only place in the country where sports betting is legal, nearly everyone uses an illegal bookie. They're a part of life, bookies are, like insurance and taxes. You hate to contribute to their cause, but let's face it, you appreciate their service.

Yet how many people know exactly how a bookie works? We know the thrill of covering the spread on a last-minute field goal and the heartbreak of seeing a three-team parlay expire on a fluke penalty. But how does the world of sports wagering look from the other side, the bookmaker's perspective?

To guys like Bobby (like other names in this story, a pseudonym), who, along with his college buddies, runs the dingy New York office, the view couldn't be better. "I work about four hours a day. I make a bundle. And there's no heavy lifting." With about 200 regular clients—including some of Manhattan's most respected, upstanding professionals—his office books more than $350,000 a week in bets.

Some operations take horse bets, but most rely on frequently televised sports. In fact, betting popularity is almost directly proportional to the amount of television coverage. Thus, hockey attracts few bettors; baseball, with its relatively complicated odds, garners about twice as many, peaking during the World Series; basketball draws about twice as many gamblers as baseball, climaxing during the NCAA championships and the NBA playoffs. But football, with its omnipresent seasonal broadcasts, easily generates the most action.

During the latter stages of a football season, when addicted gamblers are vainly chasing their losses and casual bettors have spotted spurious "trends," volume can surpass $500,000 per weekend. Culminating with Super Bowl Sunday, by far the year's biggest wagering day, Bobby's office can process nearly $10 million in football bets a year. Working with about a 5% edge, minus minuscule business expenses—rent and eight phone lines with tape recorders attached to verify bets—this bookmaking operation could easily clear twice Bill Clinton's salary.

But it doesn't. It makes much more.

The old-school bookie—the bartender at the corner saloon, the car dealer with the weekly poker game in his basement—earned his money strictly on commission. On straight bets, winners were paid even money, while losers paid 11-10, known as the "juice" or "vigorish." Business was simple: Book $100 on the Bears and $100 on the Lions and you were guaranteed to win $10. If the accounts got severely out of balance—$500 on the Bears, $180 on the Lions—old-timers simply laid off the imbalance to a wholesaler (another bookie who took larger wagers) and locked in a profit. Like most businesses, the key to success by the old method was volume. Bookies hoped for lines that would induce equal wagering on both sides—results that made half their customers winners one week and losers the next—and a never-ending stream of cash-rich players. Then they sat back and collected their "commission."

"We used to live in Harlem," one well-known professional poker player recalls. "Then my dad started making book. We moved to Long Island six months later."

The new breed of bookie, like Bobby and his cohorts, eschews the predictable collect-your-commission-and-play-it-safe methodology. If the bookies of yore were strictly brokers, content to leave the gambling to their customers, then today's bookmaker is a trader who lives by the golden rule of making money: Buy low and sell high.

"When I first started, I thought you always tried to keep your books perfectly balanced," Bobby explains. "No risk. Of course, there's much less reward. In our office, and I would say the majority of offices around the country, we don't try to balance our totals. Our feeling is, in the long run, the vig will take care of us."

In other words, most modern bookies are willing to gamble—with an edge. It's the same concept that keeps the air-conditioning flowing in the 3,000-room hotels of Las Vegas. Some days the bookmakers lose. In fact, about half the time. (Bobby's office lost nearly $100,000 during the first week of the 1994 NFL season.) But when he wins—again, about half the time—he earns 11-10 on his wagers. Factoring in the vig, the player must win his bets about 52.5% of the time just to break even. Thus, most bettors lose, since the average sports bettor will play precisely *until* he loses his bankroll. And because there are only a handful of bettors in the United States capable of consistently beating the odds in the long run, the bookie, thanks to the laws of probability, must inevitably prosper.

Fact is, some players are winners. The bookies know who they are, and when one of their bets comes in, the bookies take heed.

"When we get a bet from Clyde in Las Vegas, our office goes nuts," Bobby explains. "Within ten minutes we'll get dozens of players all going the same way as Clyde. People hear which way he's going and they want to jump on the bandwagon. In the short period of time between Clyde's bet and all the other calls is when we make our money."

What his office does, Bobby explains, is a common practice among bookies called "scalping." For example, as soon as Clyde calls in his bet on the Packers, giving six points to the Rams, Bobby gets on the phone to other bookies around New York (and sometimes the country), placing substantial bets on the Pack minus six. In the meantime, he adjusts the betting line at his office, making Green Bay a seven-point favorite. When the anticipated onslaught of calls come in following Clyde's lead, the bettors must pay a premium price. By kickoff, the Packers might be laying eight points.

"Buy cheap, sell expensive," Bobby says, grinning.

* * *

Bookies need constant infusions of fresh capital to be able to withstand the inevitable bad week. Bobby says it's crucial to constantly recruit new players and to keep the old ones he has content, even as they're bleeding off money. "That's one reason we have a five-thousand-dollar limit on any one bet. We don't want our customers going broke. We need to do a volume business."

Most bookmaking offices are organized like a pyramid. The clerks who answer the phones start out earning an hourly wage; for each new player they bring to the company they get a small percentage of the client's losses. Managers and, ultimately, the office boss get progressively larger pieces. In turn, the entire office may be part of a larger syndicate, in which case the earnings go to an unseen authority, who probably has never met the low-level clerks who answer the phones and supply him with fresh meat.

"Being a part of a large organization, a syndicate, helps you absorb the big losses," Bobby says. "But the only way to make real money is to have your own clients." To that end, Bobby and his crew frequent New York City sports bars and cardrooms. They take day trips to Atlantic City and Foxwoods in Ledyard, Connecticut. "That's one of the drawbacks of this business: You can't advertise. So you go where gamblers congregate," Bobby says. "And you dig up customers."

The majority of a bookie's business, however, finds him. "Ninety percent of our customers are referrals," Bobby reports. "If one of our regular players will vouch for a new player, we'll take his action. Maybe he has to put the cash up front for the first couple of weeks, or the guy who brought him might be responsible for anything his pal might lose. But if he comes with a recommendation, we'll take him." If the fledgling bettor proves reliable, making good on several weeks of losses, his credit limit gets raised. "We're like American Express," jokes Bobby.

Occasionally the bookmaker will get stiffed by a deadbeat. According to nearly a dozen bookies I spoke with, the party line is: "We don't use hired goons." Kneecap-breaking gorillas in shiny suits are, it seems, bad for business. "If someone holds out on me," says Raymond, one of the biggest bookies in Texas, "I write it off as a business loss. And I'm more mad at myself than anyone else for trusting the bastard."

In lieu of smashed patellas, many bookies find the best way to collect is by threatening to call the wife. "Most guys are more scared of the missus than a couple of cracked ribs," Raymond says. Like a bank, the bookmaker would rather do prior rigorous credit checks than engage in messy collection procedures.

Says Bobby, "The last thing we want to do is draw undue attention to our office over a few thousand dollars. A couple of times out of a hundred you might get screwed. That's probably the biggest downside in making book."

Well, almost. The largest liability, of course, is that it's illegal. Several weeks before the start of the 1993 NFL football season, the U.S. Attorney's office in San Francisco cracked what it believed to be the largest bookmaking ring in America. Using wiretaps, informants, and IRS records, the feds secured a 59-count grand-jury indictment against 26 members of a bookmaking syndicate that, the government said, took in roughly $1 billion a year from more than 10,000 bettors. These bookies face felony charges of racketeering, money laundering, and conspiracy.

Bobby claims he's not worried. "We're small potatoes compared to a lot of other guys. Sure, the cops could bust us if they wanted to, probably. But they've got bigger fish to fry. I've heard some of my colleagues say the over/under is four. If there are less than four people working in your office, it's a misdemeanor. More, a felony. It makes sense. The bigger the office, the bigger the bust."

None of the bookies I spoke with has ever been charged with a felony. In fact, only one of them had even been arrested. Ricky, a 20-year veteran of the business who works in a rural area of the South, has been collared four times. On each occasion he was charged with promoting gambling (a misdemeanor), fined $500, and given a suspended sentence.

Still, Bobby has contingency plans. "We're prepared," he claims. His crew rents an alternate apartment, vacant except for pre-installed phone lines. "If we get busted, we move."

He's more concerned about making the weekly exchange of cash with his clients. "Walking around New York with twenty thousand in hundred dollar bills tucked into your shorts—that's the scary part. Besides that, I don't really worry. In fact," he says, smiling widely, "since I started making book I never had it so good."

But not as good as Kelly.

Except for the cellular phone perpetually pinned to his ear, he appears to be a reputable citizen, a civic-minded pillar of his Southwestern community. And in many ways he is: The school playground boasts a shiny red fire truck he donated; the kiddie soccer league plays in smart new uniforms he provided; and the library contains enough personal computers to start a small design firm, thanks to Kelly's beneficence.

But Kelly has his dark side. Whenever he goes to Las Vegas, he regularly wins and loses six figures at the poker tables. He bets $50,000 on one roll of the dice. And when he makes a blackjack bet, it's usually at the casino's highest limit. Granted, if he wins or loses $250,000 over a weekend, it doesn't have much effect on his lifestyle. Because Kelly, pillar of his community, is probably America's biggest bookie.

Working in a syndicate with four well-capitalized partners, Kelly takes the bets no one else will handle. When bookies around the country need to get a bet down, they call Kelly. The minimum wager he accepts is $10,000— "Anything else is too messy," he deadpans—and the maximum is whatever Kelly feels comfortable with.

"I generally don't like to take more than two hundred thousand on any one game, unless it's the Super Bowl, where all the information is totally out in the open. During the regular season, too many things can happen that I don't hear about in time. Maybe ten minutes before the kickoff of a nothing game, the quarterback's wife has a miscarriage. Maybe the coach decided he's going to give his second-stringer a lot of playing time."

Though Kelly won't reveal how much he handles on a typical NFL weekend, other bookies who bet with him estimate his volume at $6 million to $7 million. Multiply that by 16 regular season games and add in the playoffs, and you've got a bookie who can afford a few soccer uniforms.

Because the numbers he deals with are so large and, in practice, so unwieldy—carrying around $100,000 bricks in a suitcase is not easy—Kelly settles only two or three times a year, flying to Chicago or Miami or Seattle to rendezvous with clients. Or he'll often use a "clearing man," a broker who arranges money transfers between two cities for a 5% commission. Other times he'll simply say, "Give it to me when you see me." Which is a particularly gentlemanly thing to do when the price of a three-bedroom house is at stake.

"Honor," Kelly says, "is a big part of this business. So is trust. There are a lot of very fine people who make book, and a lot of decent people who bet with us. Very fine individuals. It's just too bad it's illegal."

17

Risky Business

Bob Hamman has a talent for figuring out probabilities. He can do it on almost anything, really. Not only pure mathematical propositions—for example, the odds of picking the one winning key that starts a Cadillac from a bowl of 1,000 identical losers—but strange and delightful propositions that aren't necessarily subject to the laws of multiplication and division. Like the odds of a sports fan picked at random being able to make a half-court basketball shot to win $1 million. Or the chances of radio listeners in Tucson, Arizona, finding one specific, predetermined dollar bill somewhere in the city. Or the likelihood that the world record in the long jump will be broken at the Olympic Games.

You might say Bob Hamman is good with numbers. You get that way when, for 14 of the past 15 years, you've been the number-one-ranked contract bridge player on the planet and a nine-time World Champion.

"You have to have some special gifts at bridge to be at the very top," says investment maven Warren Buffet, another guy who's pretty good with numbers. "When you play with someone like Bob Hamman, they can look like they're having a drink or eating a sandwich, but they'll know everything that's going on."

When he's parked at a card table, Bob Hamman definitely knows what's going on.

This, however, is not a story about a gifted card player, a man who plays the devilishly difficult game of bridge like Tiger Woods plays golf.

It's the story of how a gifted card player exploits his powerful analytical skills, merges those talents with a profound understanding of odds and probabilities, and creates a multi-million-dollar company unique in the world of "risk management," as the insurance business is euphemistically known. It is the story of how a gifted card player figured out a clever—and profitable—way to gamble with an edge.

Bob Hamman is the man behind many of the "million-dollar challenges" you see at half-time of nationally televised sports events. And hole-in-one contests. And scratch-and-win promotions on the inside of the label of your soda bottle. Anywhere there's chance involved, whether it's the likelihood of someone finding a winning game ticket at a fast-food restaurant or redeeming a rebate coupon or shooting a hockey puck into a three-inch slot, Bob Hamman is often "booking" the bet. He—and his insurance-company investors—are the House.

His company, SCA Promotions, has covered more than $10 billion worth of potential awards and paid out more than $50 million in claims since 1986.

"Bridge and our promotions business—they're a very good fit," Hamman says, sitting in the conference room of his Dallas office. "Very similar. But business is less harsh. In bridge, when you miscalculate, you can cost yourself the match. It's over. On the other hand, when we look at some of the propositions we cover, they have enough analogous characteristics that we can make a good educated guess and hope we're not too stupid. If we estimate something has a ten percent chance of occurring and the real chance is twenty percent, it's not going to kill us," Hamman explains. "It's when we're just plain *wrong* that hurts."

Thanks to years of experience in both the gambling and insurance worlds, Bob Hamman isn't wrong very often. His company is constantly asked to evaluate peculiar risk propo-sitions—a world record "cow-chip" toss, a PGA Tour rookie winning a major championship, players on an American League baseball team hitting back-to-back-to-back home runs—and come up with a number that makes sense both for the bettor and the bookie.

"Bookie," in this sense, refers to the institution fading the bet, taking the risk. In almost every big-money sweep-stakes or contest in the world, that means an insurance com-pany. Multi-national corporations are in the business of sell-ing *things*, not gambling. When a marketing executive at a major corporation—Anheuser-Busch, for example—wants to add sizzle and heat to a prize-giveaway campaign with-out having to explain to the bean counters why his gim-mick has cost the company $2 million, he turns to SCA Pro-motions. For a fixed, fractional cost—usually less than 50¢ on the dollar—SCA and its network of insurers sweat the results.

"We sell anxiety pills," Hamman remarks. "Our cus-tomers buy time and accountability by paying us to take the heat on a proposition. In the long term, we have a posi-tive expectation. But most customers don't care about that. That doesn't make them feel better when they've got to pay off a million-dollar claim if somebody gets lucky. By using us, they take themselves off the hook. In gambling terms, they're reducing their variance."

If this all sounds eerily like casino talk, there's a reason. When you scrape away the pretty pictures about market-ing and promoting and budgeting, Bob Hamman's busi-ness is an utterly ingenious and perfectly legal way to book bets. Indeed, when a professional gambler hears about what SCA Promotions has wrought, he usually shakes his head, emits a pained groan, and says, "That's brilliant! Why didn't I think of that?"

Probably because an insurance company thought of it first. Insurance companies are society's most successful (le-gal) bookies. Every time you buy insurance, you're betting the insurer that something—a car accident, a fire in the base-

157

ment, walking pneumonia—will happen. Insurance companies are betting you it won't happen. The premium they charge, based on actuarial tables ("the odds"), figures in enough profit ("the juice") to build office towers and prop up the stock market.

Insurance companies, in case you haven't noticed, tend to make money. So do casinos. The reason is simple: When you start a proposition with what gamblers call "the best of it," in other words, a mathematical advantage, you will end up a winner over the long run. Insurance companies get themselves into the long run by writing policies for millions of people. Casinos get into the long run by conducting millions of trials every day on their tables and machines. In both arenas, the result is the same: The side with the best of it eventually takes down the dough. Sure, they have short-term losses—a hurricane hits Florida; a slot machine spits out two $1 million jackpots in a week—but the advantageous odds tend to keep the light bill paid and the corporate jet filled with fuel and good Scotch.

Of his built-in advantage, Hamman comments, "Sure, one of our clients could say, 'Hamman, you horse thief, you want to charge me five-thousand dollars for a realistic exposure of two-thousand dollars on a hundred-thousand-dollar risk! I should do it myself!' But when it gets hit for a hundred grand, none of those numbers seem to matter," he says, chuckling. "Our clients avoid 'gambler's ruin' by amortizing their risk. They're more concerned about what our promotion does for them than its true worth. It's like a computer chip. The mark-up is enormous, but you're not necessarily paying for what it costs to make; you're paying for what it can do."

For his part, Hamman says the edge SCA plays with varies. On high-volume propositions, he'll generally work with a 5%-10% advantage. On pure math or screwball propositions (like the radio station that promised its listeners $1 million if they could find Elvis Presley alive), he'll work on a paper-thin margin. "I like to work on propositions where there's no payoff," he says, laughing. "Of course, there's sometimes hidden risks, which we fail to see, as well as 'the dumb-ass factor.' Which is when we just make a foolish mistake."

That happens, he says, maybe once in 100 propositions. For example, an organization called the World Pumpkin Federation bought a contract from SCA one August that would pay $50,000 if someone in its association could grow a world-record 1,000-pound pumpkin. "They usually buy these policies in April, when the damn pumpkin is a seed," Hamman says. "Somehow it slipped past us that in this particular year they waited until near the end of the growing season."

As sure as a man's dog will start singing the "Ode to Joy" after you bet him that such a feat is impossible, the World Pumpkin Federation produced a jack-o'-lantern the size of a Volkswagen. "For all I know the pumpkin may have *lost* weight after we covered it. We made a fifty-thousand-dollar donation to that particular cause," Hamman says, chortling.

Even accounting for the occasional blunder, the odds in this business tend to take care of themselves. When you pay out, say, 5,000-to-1 on a hole-in-one when the true chances are something like 12,000-to-1, your accounts usually finish well in the black. Like the typical casino, what really hurts a company like SCA Promotions isn't a spot of bad luck, but an attack of the cheats. Hamman recalls being stung once by a claim on a half-court basketball shot that was faked by the policyholder, complete with a desktop-published newspaper account of the "winning" shot.

To filter out such shenanigans, SCA employs a director of claims and security, Norman Back. He's a former policeman, insurance man, and accomplished card mechanic who can sniff out security breaches like a pig on the trail of white truffles. "I'm a paid cynic," Back says. "I'm here to make sure the contest is as honest as possible. They try to bring me in *before* the deal is made. And when that's not possible, I review every claim before a check is cut."

On the day I visit the SCA offices, Back is watching a

black-and-white surveillance videotape shot at a college gymnasium. Several dozen fans are trying to throw a paper airplane from one of the end lines into a garbage can at half-court. (Yes, SCA will book almost *anything*.) "First I assess the environment," Back explains. "The venue looks good. There's a large audience in the arena. If it were empty, that would send up a red flag. Then I look at the conditions of the event. Do they meet the criteria we've agreed upon? The distance the airplane must be thrown, the type of paper, that sort of thing. It all checks out."

Back watches a second tape from another angle. In slow motion, he follows the progress of one shooter—the eventual winner—from entrance to exit. It's like seeing spy footage, only what's at stake here is a $10,000 prize, not our nation's future. Back watches the contest once more at full speed. "Everything's fine. It's a pay."

As much as Hamman jokes that he likes propositions that don't require a payoff, the fact that SCA *does* pay regularly, often, and well is the company's best marketing strategy. To continue the casino metaphor: If a riverboat in your area were to set its slot machines to pay out at, say, 83% while every other casino had 93% machines, gamblers would soon start avoiding the riverboat, if only for empirical reasons. SCA's reputation for promptly making good on its obligations has earned the company a lengthy client list that includes professional sports franchises (Chicago White Sox; Cleveland Indians), Fortune 500 companies (Miller Brewing, Sony Electronics), and even Las Vegas casinos (Tropicana, Boulder Station) that want to budget the unbudgetable—like a $10 million jackpot promotion.

In the past few years, SCA has developed several new lines in the re-insurance business. The company has a separate telecard division that markets pre-paid phone cards at a super-cheap price (2¢-3¢ per minute), which consumer-product manufacturers can offer as prizes or mail-in rebates. SCA's profit margin is contingent on accurately calculating the redemption rate of these little pieces of plastic. In other words, they have to do what they do best: competently analyze the inherent risk.

Another of SCA's recent innovations is insuring performance bonuses for professional athletes. For instance, a major golf-club manufacturer has agreed to pay one of its endorsers a $500,000 bonus if he wins the Masters using the manufacturer's equipment—but that half-million would bust their marketing budget. So it goes to SCA, which covers the prize for pennies on the dollar. Now the clubmaker can root wholeheartedly for its endorser to conquer Augusta, because Bob Hamman is sweating the bill.

Hamman's son, Chris, SCA's director of risk management, computes nearly every proposition that the company covers, including all of the performance bonuses. His tools are an enormous database, a keen understanding of math, and that great handicapper's attribute, personal observation.

"I don't play a lick of golf. But I like to watch," he says. Chris Hamman can tell you with near mathematical certainty what the chances are that Phil Mickelson will win a major championship this year; what the odds are of Davis Love winning back-to-back majors; how likely it is for Jim Furyk to win *any* tournament. Of the fan-from-the-stands promotions, he can assure you that the half-court basketball shot is a little harder than you might think, the 10-foot putt is even harder, and the field-goal kick is actually the least difficult of them all.

How does he know? "Nothing beats experience," he says, smiling. "After you've paid out a few six-figure checks, you get a pretty good feel for these things."

Golf, tennis, hockey, motor sports, even professional bass fishing—SCA covers them all. When your favorite race-car driver wins a $1 million bonus or your hometown right-winger breaks the NHL scoring record, the guy wincing in his office is Bob Hamman.

But don't worry about old Bob. He's got the Edge on his side—and we all know what that does for the typical bookie. Or world-champion bridge player. Or multi-billion-dollar insurance company.

18

The Biggest Game
of the Year

You know you're going to bet on it.

Even if you promise the wife you won't, even if you swear to your buddies at the office that you're not going to get financially involved, that you're going to sit back with a cold brew and merely watch the Big One—you're still going to bet on the Super Bowl.

Who doesn't? You hear as many estimates on how much is gambled on the Bowl as there are opinions about "Who's The Best Quarterback In The NFL?" The most common figure: $5 billion. That's a lot of six-packs. No wonder every play of the game, no matter how seemingly inconsequential, makes someone very happy. Or very sad.

Whether at one of the legal sports books in Nevada, with the bookie at the corner bar, or, most likely, in the office pool, sports fans across America will make an investment in the outcome of football's ultimate clash. Most of us will have just "a little something" riding on the final score, a small slice of pie that makes the game taste noticeably sweeter when our chosen team wins. Some of us will have a shot at parlaying our $5 pool bet into several hundred. And some—those of us who think we know something, as well as those who definitely don't know anything but are looking for one last chance to make up for a season of bad betting decisions—will be wagering far more than the bank balance warrants.

The Super Bowl produces great plays, great players, great memories. It also produces some of the best betting stories you've ever heard. Here are three of the greatest.

Right Down the Middle: 1979

It's every bettor's dream. And in the history of the Super Bowl, it has happened only once.

Only in 1979 did the unthinkable occur: The bookies got "middled."

Bookmakers generally try to keep their accounts balanced, attracting a like amount of money on both teams. (On a huge event like the Super Bowl, where a single Las Vegas sports book will take in millions, keeping the action "even" and minimizing exposure to catastrophic losses is especially important.) With a perfectly balanced book, the casinos are assured of a profit, thanks to the vig, the 11-10 juice gamblers must pay. To achieve perfectly balanced accounts—or as close as they can get—the bookies adjust the point spread, moving the line up or down to attract bets to the side that's getting less support. It's like any market: When the price goes down, people tend to buy more. But if the line moves too much, tragedy—or comedy, depending on your perspective—can strike.

In 1979, the Steelers were initially favored by 2 1/2 points over the Cowboys. Everyone in the world bet on Pittsburgh, laying the points, figuring the men in black to win by at least a field goal.

To stimulate action on the Cowboys, bookies raised the line to 3 points. Still, the public bet the Steelers. With their accounts getting seriously imbalanced, the bookmakers were forced to notch up the point spread another half-point, making Pittsburgh a 3 1/2 point favorite. A little money started to trickle in on the Cowboys, but even more came in on the Steelers. The bookies were starting to feel the heat of lopsided action.

So again they upped the line, to 4. And then 4 1/2. Finally

the bookmakers got the desired effect: Money began to flow in on Dallas. By kickoff, with Dallas getting 4 1/2 points, the accounts weren't exactly balanced, but they weren't seriously skewed either. A monumental multi-million-dollar disaster had been averted.

Or so they thought.

Twenty-two seconds after the Cowboys' Butch Johnson caught a four-yard touchdown pass from Roger Staubach, the game ended with a score of 35-31—the Steelers by four. Everyone who had bet on the Steelers up to -3 1/2 won; everyone who took the Cowboys +4 or +4 1/2 won or tied (and had their wager returned). Thanks to the score falling on the magic "middle" number, almost every gambler in America won their Super Bowl bet.

Except the bookies.

Bob's Big Bet: 1989

Known as the Barnum of Las Vegas, casino owner Bob Stupak, former proprietor of Bob Stupak's Vegas World, would do anything for publicity. (When Stupak suffered a near-fatal motorcycle accident shortly before the completion of his skyline-dominating Stratosphere Tower, local wags commented Bob always knew how to grab the headlines.) The man was a marketing juggernaut. If it would help fill his casino with gamblers, he'd come up with the craziest stunts.

Like betting $1 million on the Super Bowl.

San Francisco was favored by 7 points over Cincinnati. Bob liked the Bengals and the points. After arranging a preferential deal on the juice—Stupak allegedly had to lay only 21-20, instead of the standard 11-10, a $50,000 saving—Stupak bet Gene Maday's Little Caesar's sports book $1,050,000 to win $1 million.

As expected, the bet generated millions of dollars in international press coverage for Bob and his Vegas World gambling hall: "Swashbuckling Vegas casino owner takes the plunge, backs Cincinnati to the tune of a million bucks!"

At the gun, San Francisco had triumphed, 20-16. But with his 7-point cushion, Bob Stupak was $1 million richer.

Trailed by the television cameras he adored, Bob walked out of Little Caesar's with a box and a brown paper sack from McDonald's, filled presumably with bricks of hundred dollar bills.

The American public loved the story. And to this day most people remember Bob Stupak as The Guy Who Won a Million on the Super Bowl.

Only problem was, the box was empty and the brown bag contained shredded paper.

According to Las Vegan John Smith, author of the Bob Stupak biography *No Limit*, casino bosses up and down the Strip immediately scoffed at the bet's authenticity. Speculation was that Stupak faked the bet by wagering on both sides, guaranteeing himself a small loss on the juice in return for many millions of dollars in publicity.

Bob Stupak claimed the bet was on the square.

The Gaming Control Board, Smith says, inquired into the validity of the wager and found no compelling reason to doubt Stupak. "Some guys, when they have a problem with their girlfriend, go out and drink too much," Stupak told Smith. "Me, I bet too much."

The Raider Plays a Hunch: 1996

In 1996, anyone who knew anything about sports could have told you the San Francisco 49ers would beat the San Diego Chargers in Super Bowl XXX. (The bookies agreed, installing the Niners as a 19-point favorite, the biggest spread in Super Bowl history.) Short of Steve Young and Jerry Rice suffering a couple of freak leg fractures in pre-game warm-ups, no one with even a remedial understanding of what makes a football team win could have presented a case for the Chargers somehow pulling off a victory.

We all knew Super Bowl XXX was going to be a coronation party for San Francisco, the royalty of the NFL. But only one man was willing to bet a fortune on his conviction.

Shortly before game time, a man—we'll call him the Raider—approached the sports book at the Mirage casino and told one of the clerks at the counter he wanted to bet on the 49ers. No point spread, nothing fancy, just the 49ers to win, straight up. The clerk checked the tote board: San Francisco was an 8-to-1 favorite. If you wanted to bet the "money line," independent of the point spread, you'd have to lay $80 to win $10. (On the other hand, a $10 bet on the Chargers would win you $70.) The Raider nodded thoughtfully and asked to see the manager.

The boss came out and asked the Raider, "How can I help you?" The Raider told him he wanted to bet a bunch of money on San Francisco to win. How much could he bet?

"As much as you would like, sir," the manager replied.

"Good," the Raider said. "I want two million, four-hundred thousand on San Francisco."

After ascertaining that the man was serious—he already had the money on deposit in the casino cage—the manager reminded the Raider that, at 8-to-1, his $2.4 million would win him only $300,000 if San Francisco came through. "Yes, I know," the Raider said. "And, of course, they *will* win."

And, yes, they did, spanking San Diego 49-26.

The next morning, the Las Vegas papers carried stories about an anonymous gambler making a huge bet on the Niners. The sports book manager at the Mirage said he didn't mind taking the Raider's $2.4 million bet and subsequently paying off the $300,000 win, since, the bookmaker said, the guy helped balance the Mirage's books.

For months the identity of the shadowy gambler with *cojones* the size of football helmets remained a mystery. Whispers floated around town like so many tumbleweeds in the desert.

Months later, the *Las Vegas Advisor,* a savvy local newsletter, confirmed what wiseguy gamblers had known from the start: Losing $2.4 million on the Super Bowl wasn't going to drastically change the man's life, just as $300,000 would hardly raise his pulse. Like all the rest of us football fans around America, billionaire corporate raider Carl Icahn just wanted a little extra something riding when he watched the biggest game of the year.

19

1-900-NFL-SCAM

David James is a 30-year-old man who, to be honest, doesn't know much about football. He knows of course what a first down is and which team won the Super Bowl last year, and all that. But he'll freely admit he's no expert. Like most casual football fans, David James couldn't tell you which AFC club has the best defensive line against the run or which NFC coach gives his team a day off after close wins or what indoor stadium produces the highest-scoring playoff contests. And like most casual football fans who wager in the office football pool and bet with the local bookie, he certainly couldn't possibly predict which teams will cover the point spread and win the money.

So why did hundreds of gamblers spend more than $60,000 during the 1993 football season to hear David James' NFL selections?

Because David James, a guy who doesn't know much about football, knows a lot about marketing.

"I run a nationwide executive search firm," he tells me. "Everything about the recruiting business is perception." We're sitting in the conference room of his modest suite of offices in Temecula, California. Two large oil portraits of his children, who also don't know much about football, dominate the wall behind him. He's thin and tall and wears glasses. He's nice looking. Smart. Yet I cannot perceive anything about David James that would compel me to give him $25 to tell me who will win the Cowboys-Vikings game.

"Back in nineteen-ninety, ninety-one, I would see these advertisements on television and in *The National* [the now-defunct national sports daily] promoting nine-hundred-lines manned by 'top handicappers' and 'betting experts'—complete nonsense. Every week they claimed to have killed the bookies. Every week they were big winners. *You couldn't lose with these guys.* I asked myself, what makes them better at picking football winners than me? Nothing, of course. It's all the perception.

"Some of these guys had eight-hundred-lines, which gave you quotes on prices. I'd call the eight-hundred-line and ask the analysts what exactly it was that made them an expert," he recalls, chuckling. "They would say they had four-hundred advance scouts on their payroll, fifty years in the business. All sorts of hilarious crap. Well, I decided then that I had to be just as much of an expert."

David James figured if these heavily promoted charlatans could command $10 to $25 (and sometimes more for "Games of the Year!") per three-minute 900-line call, he could too. "This is a country where people read the *National Enquirer* and *The Weekly World News* and believe a woman gave birth to a hundred-pound baby," he says, smiling. "Why shouldn't they believe me?"

With merely three weeks of investigative research for ammunition, in 1991 James decided to take a shot at the 900-line handicapping business. Advertising himself as "Harv Edwards: America's Best Sports Analyst" (Harv's voice provided courtesy of an office-mate), James says he grossed nearly $4,000 a week during football season from a $200-a-week advertisement in *The National*. "My buddy and I just picked the games off the top of our heads. I think we were right about half the time," James says, shrugging innocently. Then *The National*, the sports bettor's bible, closed. James turned to advertising on sports radio in 1992, but barely broke even. Harv Edwards was forced into early retirement.

For David James, however, the experiment was an epiphany. He had discovered how the 900-line handicapping business works. "In those first two football seasons I learned a lot of powerful stuff," he tells me, nodding his head conspiratorially.

"Such as…"

"Such as, the more you charge, the better they think you are. Such as, nobody *ever* asks for documentation of the claims made in your advertisements. Such as, the clientele for a 900-line that purports to be able to pick winners in a football game is so sick that even if you *lose* they won't stop calling you. If you win, great! They love you. You're a genius. And if you happen to lose… They figure you can't be wrong twice, so they call you again, get the next game, and double their bet. Thursday night ESPN game, they bet a hundred dollars and lose. Saturday morning college, two-hundred dollars; afternoon game, four-hundred dollars. Now they're probably stuck close to a grand. Sunday morning NFL, maybe they bet three games at three hundred apiece, all based on my predictions. Then sometimes another grand on the late game. And then, if they're still stuck, the big bailout game. I got more calls for the Monday night game than all the other games combined."

James also found that certain phrases held a special resonance with football bettors: "Sure Thing!" "Lock of the Decade!" "Guaranteed Winner!" Anything compulsive plungers could believe was luckier or wiser or better than they. Any shred of hope on which to cling.

"And if this game doesn't come through for you," James says, in his best pitchman's voice, "you get the entire playoffs…" He takes a deep breath and yells, "…ABSOLUTELY FREE!"

In 1993, without Harv Edwards to provide the answers, James needed a new gimmick, a way to get eager gamblers to call him and not another "sure thing" sports service. He noticed that many of his competitors' lines promoted themselves on the longevity platform: "We've been around this game so long, we must know something!" Rather than try to out-old the "old-timers" (mostly guys in their 30s and 40s, actually), James took the contrarian approach.

Using a high-school-reunion photograph that made him look like a cross between a youthfully bespectacled Big Six CPA and a hopelessly bookish nerd, David James began advertising himself in national sports betting publications as "The Wiz Kid: Bookies *hate* him! You will *love* him!" Immediately the phones began to ring.

Without explicitly saying so, the Wiz Kid ad implied there was a new hotshot on the scene, a precocious fresh handicapping talent who used new-fangled methods the old-timers couldn't even imagine. The word "computer" never appeared in any of the Wiz Kid's promotional material, but everything about James' smiling, freshly scrubbed face screamed MIT. Peering at that credible, educated, comically "intellectual" face, gamblers around America, knowing that, hey, bookies *hate* him, began to assume the Wiz Kid must have powerful software at his disposal, some sort of invincible parallel processor that crunched innumerable statistics into a quantifiable expression of gridiron prowess.

"I had my four-year-old son make the picks," David James confesses.

His advertisement, after all, promised selections from the Wiz Kid. And who better to play the role than a boy on the threshold of kindergarten?

"Every week I'd run the games by my son," James reveals. "He knew what football was but, of course, he didn't really have an opinion about point spreads. He couldn't read, he didn't know the rules, he didn't know why daddy was asking him, but he liked to play the game every week. I'd say, 'Hey, Daniel, which team's going to win, Chicago or Green Bay.' He'd point at the newspaper. The team he picked went on the line. I'd just make up some bogus statistic to justify his selection: wind conditions on the field—you know, stuff that was totally uncheckable. The first week he went 1-7. The next week he was 8-0. My call volume tripled."

By the fourth week of the NFL season, Daniel was maintaining an astonishing 70% success rate. Each week the Wiz Kid's call volume, at $25 a shot, continued to double. In the 10th week of the season Daniel again went 8-0; business soared. During the Wiz Kid's peak, gamblers around America had approximately $150,000 a week in wagers riding on the four-year-old's "advice." And as James had discovered, even when Daniel had losing streaks, volume remained constant. By season's end his average was a respectable—and profitable—56% (52.5% is break even), precisely 6% better than you could expect flipping a nickel.

By playoff time, though, David James had stopped advertising his service. "I couldn't do it anymore," he says sheepishly, almost ashamed to admit that he quit. According to James he discontinued his Wiz Kid line, not because of the death threat he received after losing his "Game of the Year!" ("That happens all the time in this business," he says matter-of-factly) and not because the pathos of his addicted clients kept him up at night. "Irony of ironies, I felt responsible for getting all these people even. It became a crusade for me: How am I going to get this customer his new Mercedes back? How am I going to win enough to get that customer's seventy-six-thousand-dollar debt forgiven? I got sucked into the game emotionally—just like a degenerate gambler!"

The $25,000 James says he netted from his son pointing at the sports section surely helped salve the psychic wounds. Yet James insists he no longer has any interest in promoting a 900-handicapping line. The Wiz Kid has grown up, so to speak. "This may sound funny, but I'm trying to operate on a higher plane, where the energy you put out, the positive energy, comes back to you. You know, karma. So…" He stares wistfully at his son's portrait on the conference room wall. The expression on David James' face just then is very much like what you see on the face of a Las Vegas gambler who's tapped out his line of credit.

Poker

20

Shakin' Down
the Sheiks

"The basic idea behind coming all the way to Africa to play in a poker tournament is this: Anyone we haven't seen before, we can beat. It's really simple as that. If I don't know them, I'm better than them."

Eric Drache, the former poker room manager of the Mirage, is holding court at Cairo's Casino Shehrazade, site of the inaugural King Tut International Poker Tournament. Accompanied by an all-star contingent of professional gamblers that includes some of America's best card players, Drache has journeyed to Egypt in search of the Big Score—that bulging pot of easy money at the end of every professional gambler's rainbow. In previous years, the Big Score has had Drache and his pals roaming the planet like jackals in search of fresh meat, trekking from Malta to Morocco, Australia to Austria, hoping to find opponents willing to play poker for virtually any stakes, particularly guys whose card-playing skills are blissfully smaller than their bloated bankrolls.

"We don't give a damn about their politics or their religion," says Drache, "and we really have no respect for their money. Poker is a great equalizer."

One September not long ago, the high rollers were hoping the Big Score would come from someone who looks roughly like Yasir Arafat, owns an oil field or three, and has not the slightest qualm about wagering sums approaching the average American's yearly salary on a card game he barely understands. In other words, a fun-lovin' "A-rab."

"The whole key to winning at poker is playing someone you're better than," Drache explains. "You might be the ten-millionth best player in the world, but if you're playing the eleven millionth, you'll win. Of course, it helps to be in the top fifty."

Eric Drache knows something about this topic. Back in 1982, the now-defunct *Gambling Times* ranked him the sixth-best seven-card stud player in the world. "His trouble," they said then, "is that he only plays with the top five." So for someone like Drache, who has a notorious reputation for digging himself into deep holes of debt, plunking down $3,750 for the King Tut Tournament's package deal is a worthwhile investment, if only to escape the all-too-familiar faces of his Vegas creditors.

Here Drache is one of several dozen Americans, including a crack crew of imported dealers and floor personnel, encamped across the street from the Pyramids of Giza at the Mena House Oberoi Hotel, Cairo's finest digs. Originally a hunting lodge favored by Egyptian royalty, the Mena House is now slathered in crystal and rosewood and gold, and is home to a casino where Saudi sheiks routinely stop by to donate $50,000 at the roulette wheel. The chief, if unstated, motive behind the King Tut Tournament is to intercept those very same sheiks (and their petro-dollars) before they scuttle back to their harems.

Because of strict Islamic law, gambling is, of course, forbidden in virtually every Arab state. Egypt, however, is a progressive exception. But even gentlemen who subscribe to the notion that if you don't believe in Allah, you ain't shiite, need to have some fun.

The tournament organizers, Nagy Younan, a former Las Vegas poker dealer turned fledgling entrepreneur, and John Hall, the Casino Shehrazade's British manager, hope to provide an interesting diversion for the sheiks, a delightful

challenging interlude filled with camaraderie, sportsman-
ship, and good cheer. In other words, a poker game in which
the American pros can take the Middle Easterners for all
they're worth.

By the end of the first day of the scheduled 10-day ex-
travaganza, it becomes clear to the Americans that the tournament will live up to its international billing, at least. There
are five poker-playing emissaries from Germany, England,
and Nepal. There are card sharks with strange accents from
Allah-knows-where. And there's even a handful of players
who meet Drache's unfamiliarity test, like the tax dodger
from the Isle of Man and the importer-exporter of some
mysterious commodity who resides somewhere in the West-
ern Hemisphere.

Unfortunately for the Americans, though, there aren't
many faces from the Persian Gulf. Indeed, by 10 p.m., when
most Middle Eastern big shots have yet to finish dinner, a
general uneasiness over the dearth of sheiks has already
permeated the casino floor. Dealers fidget at empty tables.
The floor personnel fiddle with the studs on their tuxedos.
And the Americans, clad in track suits and gold chains,
huddle in expectant anxious clumps. Manning Briggs, a
voluble Texan who has come strictly for the side games
(where the action is 10 times as big as the tournament, with
its modest entry fee of $500) tells the group, "I just want to
see someone walk in here wearing a robe!"

Reacting quickly, John Hall assures the anxious pros
that several members of the Kuwaiti royalty regularly drop
in to gamble away their fortunes. "They'll be here," he says,
smiling. "They'll be here."

Or maybe not. Out of the players' earshot, Hall tells me
of 20 punters from Great Britain who canceled on short
notice. "They inquired about attending, but they were
doubtful as to the seriousness of the activities. I gave them
a list of the Americans scheduled to compete. Apparently,
they decided it was a bit *too* serious."

Waiting for a fellow named Achmed or Abdul to show
up, the Americans amuse themselves with a friendly little

game of $50-$100 Dealer's Choice—mostly hold 'em and seven-card stud, with pots routinely in the $2,000 neighborhood, chicken feed to this gang. Several minutes later, a corpulent be-robed Kuwaiti waddles in. To the American players he's a wallet waiting to be emptied. Their faces rise in unison as he and his bodyguard head toward the green-baize poker tables—and then fall as he plops down at the roulette wheel. As the sheik litters the field of numbers with stacks of chips, the Americans' eyes take on the sort of glazed half-drunk quality normally found in men ogling a beautiful but unattainable woman. The drooling is almost audible as the Kuwaiti proceeds to lose several grand in about four minutes.

Dozens of accusing eyes turn toward the Tut's organizers. Mutiny seems imminent; rebellion is at hand. And then, as if delivered by Mohammed himself, the Moustache makes his entrance.

He is fully costumed in a flowing white *galabia,* with a matching *challah* wrapped around his head. His hands are thin and delicate, his eyes dark and filled with amusement. In softly murmured Arabic, the Kuwaiti "businessman"— they *all* describe themselves as a businessman of some sort— with his magnificent moustache tells one of the suddenly smiling organizers that he would like very much to play some poker.

The Moustache is escorted to one of the games in progress and is promptly seated across from a menagerie of chop-licking Americans, who can barely contain their glee when an attendant fetches the new arrival $10,000 in chips. An exotically outfitted companion sits to his side, whispering conspiratorially. The grinning Americans look at the Kuwaitis and think, "What a bunch of clowns!" The Moustache and his pal stare across the felt at Puggy Pearson's smashed-in nose and omnipresent cigar, Manning Briggs' foot-long ponytail, and Eric Drache's Beatles-meet-Henry V haircut and think, "What a bunch of clowns!" In approximately five minutes, one of the parties will quickly be disabused of that notion.

Like vultures spying a run-over rabbit, Americans from every corner of the casino dash to claim the remaining seats at the table. They suggest a $300-$600 stud game. But the shift supervisor, John "Schof" Sheffield, counsels caution and patience: "You've got to start out low," he whispers. "Those sheiks come here the first night and lose two thousand, but they have fun. So they come back the next night with five thousand and a friend. And then they come back the next night with twenty-five thousand and lose that. Hey, that's how the pyramids were built!"

So the players agree on a $25-$50 pot-limit Omaha game, a form of poker in which pots that begin as a humble pile of chips gradually grow as high as obelisks. In Omaha, each player starts with four cards in his hand and must match two of them with three of five community cards turned up on the table to make his best five-card hand. It's a poker game the Moustache says he favors, probably, the pros infer, because every hand looks good. Even the worst quartet of "rags" can end up a winner. What the Moustache apparently does *not* know is that in Omaha the edge of skill between a rank novice and an 80-hour-a-week Vegas veteran is magnified about 100 times. In the long run, as sure as a flush beats a straight, the pigeon will lose.

On the first hand dealt, the Moustache and Manning Briggs get involved in a pot. Though the Kuwaitis are paranoiacally publicity-shy, I'm able to get close enough to see that the Moustache is holding nothing. Nothing but dreams. Just a series of random, unmatched cards. And yet he's invested nearly $3,000 in the pot. Briggs, on the other hand, has two pair, aces and fours. With two cards to be dealt, the Moustache needs a miracle.

Which he duly gets. The penultimate card gives him a meager pair of queens (and more than enough motivation to toss in another $3,000); the last card—praise Allah!—is another queen, giving him three ladies or, in poker parlance, "six titties."

Upon seeing the Kuwaiti's hand revealed, most casual poker players would probably sneer and pout and utter some derogatory expletive, roll their eyes heavenward, and fling their cards at the satanic dealer. Not Briggs, though. Not even with $15,000 in the pot. The consummate pro, a man who knows that in the short term the rabbit may elude the hunter but will eventually end up stewing in a cauldron, Briggs bows his head ceremoniously and says, "Nice hand, sir. Very well played." Then he applauds lightly as the Moustache rakes in his unlikely spoils. The other players, shooting knowing glances around the table, dutifully join in, forming an obsequious claque that will shortly turn ruthless.

Two hours, 50 hands, and many thousands of dollars later, the Moustache is broke.

Two nights later another Kuwaiti swaggers into the Casino Shehrazade, itching to play some seven-card stud. The Americans gladly oblige, anointing him "the King"— as in, "of Poker"—while they systematically drain him of cash. The first night he plays, the King bets on every hand, seemingly oblivious to their relative merits, or lack thereof.

Starting with three small unmatched cards, the King tosses chips into the pot as if they were so many matchsticks. Even when it's patently apparent to everyone at the table that "Cajun Joe" Petro (from Lafayette, Louisiana) has a powerful pair of aces in his hand, the King flings away, as if desperate to rid himself of the chips stacked before him. Even when the King's meager pair of threes are up against Vegas pro Chuck Sharp's wired tens; when his inside straight draw is matched against California champ David Wight's made two pair; when the hapless Kuwaiti has, in short, brought a paper clip to a rocket-launcher fight—even *then* he continues to toss and toss away. No matter the bet—$75, $150, $300—the King plows on, intoxicated by the $4,000 pots his recklessness has helped create. Miraculously, as the sun dawns over the Sahara, he is winning.

Before it dawns the next day, he will have lost everything.

To the players' chagrin, though, this kind of fast-and-loose action occurs with disappointing infrequency. The

King shows up a few more times, as does a secretive Palestinian living in Cyprus. But the hoped-for Saudi billionaires stay away. What's worse, it's not even the Americans' fault. According to a large group of sheiks I found playing blackjack at two downtown Cairo casinos, the Middle Easterners enacted something like a group boycott of the King Tut Tournament, because the management at Casino Shehrazade does not treat them with "the proper respect." If they are going to lose their money, they say, they would at least like to get something in return. Good old-fashioned kowtowing, for example.

* * *

Deprived of the hoped-for action, the Americans find a variety of amusements. Naturally, there's plenty to do. This is Egypt, the birthplace of art and civilization. The sights are majestic, awe-inspiring, and right across the street. But to most of the players, experiencing "local culture" means catching a little belly-dancing and stuffing $10 bills in the dancer's cleavage.

What these boys like best is to gamble. On anything.

Even in Egypt, there's no escaping it. On the bus to the airport, in the 10 minutes it takes to check luggage, during a tour of the Great Temple of Amon—out come the cards. In their downtime, the Americans play golf for $100 a hole, gin rummy for $50 a box, or backgammon for several hundred bucks a point. (One well-known player loses more than $20,000 in one disastrous session.) Someone briefly considers organizing a series of camel races, but decides the outcome could be too easily fixed. Out on a shopping spree at the Khan el-Khalili bazaar, Puggy Pearson—former World Champion of Poker Puggy Pearson—happens upon a cafe filled with Egyptians smoking water pipes and playing some sort of inscrutable card game for stakes equivalent to about 30 cents. His girlfriend drags him away to shop for trinkets moments before old Pug is about to pull up a chair and make the boys a proposition. "Ah recognize the game!"

he implores, in his Tennessee drawl. "Ah know it!"

Most of the poker players have a peculiar way of investigating the nearby archaeological sites: arrive, snap a photo, leave.

One day, the group decides to rent a stable of Arabian horses and ride them across the Sahara to the Pyramids at Saqqara, site of King Zoser's Step Pyramid. After more than two hours of riding, during which two horses attempt to roll over on their poker-playing jockeys and another takes off at full gallop for its stable in Giza, the Americans arrive and, ignoring the 5,000-year-old artifacts all around them, promptly pile into taxicabs and head back to the Mena House. Later in the week, half the group disappears during a guided tour of the Egyptian Museum, home to King Tut's treasures, among many other marvels. They're eventually discovered at the Hilton, eating cheeseburgers.

Given their inescapable proximity, eventually every one of the King Tut Tournament's participants gets around to making a perfunctory pilgrimage to the Pyramids at Giza. The Pyramids are beautiful, enigmatic, eternal. They are also a constant reminder that the outcome of a poker tournament in the desert is, in the end, colossally inconsequential.

Still, the Americans would rather be gambling.

So there they are, on a five-star cruise of the Nile, heading from Luxor to Aswan. As the boat floats down the great river, the poker players are too preoccupied to notice what's passing by, though they do occasionally dash upstairs to get a peek at the topless Czechoslovakian girls lolling on the sundeck. Little Nubian boys herding hump-backed oxen; man-size slabs of granite cut out of the mountains; traditionally clad Bedouins riding skinny white donkeys; ancient tombs hidden in the hillside—all of it might as well be buried underneath the sand. The Americans are ensconced in the boat's air-conditioned lounge, busy playing seven-card stud.

21

Trump Cards

Poker tournaments are similar to PGA Tour golf events: They measure their success by the quality of the field they attract. Like the unlucky Tour stops that are scheduled opposite the British Open or Ryder Cup, struggling poker tournaments draw few players and, in turn, even fewer top players. Flourishing poker tournaments, on the other hand, draw thousands of entrants, including most of the "leading money winners," who follow the scent of available cash like vultures sniff out carrion. The presence of big-name competitors—world champions, winners of the poker "majors"—gives a poker tournament instant prestige and cachet, like when Tiger Woods or Greg Norman deign to play the Greater Milwaukee Open.

The World Series of Poker, at Binion's Horseshoe in downtown Las Vegas, draws the biggest and best field in poker. The tournament is 28 years old.

The United States Poker Championship, at the Trump Taj Mahal in Atlantic City, draws the second biggest and best field in poker. The tournament is two years old.

There are any number of plausible reasons why a fledgling poker tournament like the United States Poker Championship might draw more than 3,000 entries and pay out $4 million in prize money: the novelty of simply being something new in the world of gambling; the highly respected administrators (Jim Albrecht and Jack McClelland, who also run the World Series) directing and coordinating the action; the East Coast location.

And one other reason: a guy named Donald J. Trump attaching his name to the event.

Mr. Trump, as you must know—for he wouldn't be doing his job well if you didn't—likes Big. He likes Top. He likes Number One. So you can be sure when Donald J. Trump inaugurates the United States Poker Championship at his Trump Taj Mahal casino in 1996, the event won't be just another new tournament hoping to get its feet wet in the immense pool of money that is professional wagering. It'll be a Trump kind of thing.

Mr. Trump has an enormously developed talent for attracting television cameras, even to poker tournaments, which normally draw hapless dreamers and ruthless opportunists, not network news coverage. Thus the USPC is the kind of Trumpian spectacle where, in addition to the best poker players in the world, a young lady named Yasmine Bleeth, a cast member on the syndicated bikini-fest "Baywatch," competes for the $500,000 first prize. Though her putative assets are plain to see, her poker-playing ability is not as immediately clear. Still, in the early going of the main event, before the 10 o'clock news crews have left, before the bags under her eyes start to show through her cosmetic fortification, Yasmine Bleeth has a ton of chips. The delicious irony in all this—lost on the paparazzi and boom-mike operators—is that Ms. Baywatch, through the luck of the draw, has been randomly assigned a seat next to a gentleman named Huck Seed, who happens to be the reigning World Champion of Poker. The further irony is that he has far fewer chips than a lady whose chief talent was previously thought to be wearing a swimsuit.

Flashing a smile almost as glittering as the ornate chandeliers that hang over the Taj Mahal poker room, Ms. Bleeth tells the cameras she has never played poker before, but that it's a lot of fun to find a sport where you don't have to sweat.

Now, whether or not tournament poker is a "sport" may be open to discussion, but as far as ESPN, the arbiter in such matters, is concerned, poker qualifies. The total sports network has dispatched a large production crew to the USPC to produce an hour-long highlight show for airing after the Super Bowl. (This being the USPC's first edition, one can sense the hand of Trump at work again, garnering coverage that others might take years to procure.) ESPN has enlisted Gabe "Welcome Back, Kotter" Kaplan, himself an accomplished poker player, to do color commentary and spot interviews with the poker luminaries in attendance, including, of course, "the Girl from Baywatch," as everyone has taken to calling the player seated next to Huck Seed.

Seven other former World Champions are in the field, including Phil Hellmuth Jr. who, in contrast to Mr. Seed, steadily and surely amasses a stack of chips, cutting away at his opponents' bankrolls—and confidence—like a surgeon removing a polyp. Hellmuth raises frequently and fearlessly, forcing the competition to constantly guess: Does he? Or doesn't he? Does he have the hand he claims to have, or is he bluffing? This being a no-limit event—meaning you may bet any or all of your chips at any time—being wrong can precipitate an early exit from the tournament and a quick farewell to your $7,500 entry fee. Of the 100 contestants in the finals of the USPC, Phil Hellmuth Jr. seems best prepared to take home the half-million.

But before he does he'll have to acquire *every* chip in play. The tournament works like this: You play until you lose all your chips, and the tournament isn't over until one person has everyone else's money. The winner, in essence, has to parlay $7,500 in chips into $750,000 in chips. At the USPC the process takes three days. Winning is not so much the function of one big dramatic moment as the accumulation of hundreds of small moments, thousands of small decisions, like a sculptor chipping away at marble.

Remarkably, after the first day of play, in which 57 players are eliminated, Ms. Baywatch still remains, outlasting three World Champions, including her tablemate Huck

Seed. The effect of her five-inch heels on the luck of the cards is unclear; the effect on her competition is obvious.

But it is another woman who is making the most profound impact on the tournament. Atlantic City local Cyndy Violette, one of Donald J. Trump's personal favorites, has the second-most chips after Day One, $45,300. Only Phil Hellmuth has more. The staff of the Taj Mahal, where Violette regularly plies her trade as a high-limit poker pro, is rooting for her to make the final table.

So is Tournament Director Jim Albrecht, who tells me the presence of a woman in the top five would do wonders for this new tournament, not to mention poker in general. But even without a gender-based public relations coup, Albrecht thinks the first USPC is a startling success. "In its first year, four million dollars in prize money? That's unheard of. I'm thrilled. We've had our difficulties. The regulations in New Jersey require so much paperwork it takes a week to switch anything, including the starting time of an event. But despite the growing pains, we've set all kinds of records."

The record Albrecht—along with Poker Room Manager Tommy Gitto and everyone else connected to the tournament—is most proud of is the one set in the seven-card stud event, which draws 122 players, each of whom puts up a $4,000 entry fee. The prize pool, $513,000, is the largest for a stud event in the history of poker, larger even than the World Series of Poker. "Texas hold 'em is the most popular game back in Vegas," Albrecht says. "But stud is still king here. It's the Beast of the East. So it's appropriate, I guess, that the new world record belongs to the Taj."

Indeed, the biggest poker room in town puts on the biggest stud poker tournament in the world. In its first try. Very Trump.

When the casino magnate and consummate promoter makes himself available for 10 minutes, I see for myself why Donald J. Trump is so successful at being this oversized character known as Donald J. Trump. While a camera crew from a Fox network morning talk show is setting up its lights, we meet in the Taj Mahal's Alexander the Great penthouse suite to talk about the latest addition to Trump's gambling empire.

Me: What is your personal poker background?

Trump (staring at the gorgeous female reporter who will soon be taking my place on the couch): My life is a poker match.

Me (also staring): Are you a player?

Trump: I've never had time to play seriously. I've been too busy to really focus on poker. But my life is a series of poker games. Ins and outs. Ups and downs. Highs and lows.

Me: Is there an element of bluff?

Trump: Yes, there's an element of bluff in everything. Oftentimes you'll see great businessmen being great poker players. And a lot of the great poker players, if they were in business, would be natural businessmen.

Me: Why have you created the United States Poker Championship? Why here and now?

Trump: Here at the Taj Mahal we have a tremendous poker facility that has swept out the competition in Atlantic City, and we've become the dominant factor, the dominant place, the one place to play. Most of the big play is here. Through my own luck and talent, the poker players on the East Coast have gravitated to the Taj. The United States Poker Championship brings a lot of glamour to this venue.

Me: Why such a large commitment to poker in such a large space, a space that we both know could turn a much greater profit if it were filled with slot machines?

Trump: It costs me money. But overall it's a very positive experience. You've got every major television station down here, ESPN. It's been really terrific. I have one of the biggest slot parlors in the world, I think almost five thousand slots. Whether we add some slots, I have a level of slot machines that practically nobody in the world has, so it's not like the slot revenue is suffering. So it doesn't matter to me. Poker has been great for the facility. It's brought excitement, it's brought glamour, and it's brought a tremendous amount of people. And a lot of these people then go from poker to our baccarat tables, which, you know, is at a very high level.

Me: Where do you see this tournament going? How big can it grow?

Trump: We'll get bigger every year. I think we can become the most important poker tournament in the world. I look forward to having the biggest poker tournament in the world. And I think that will happen in the very near future.

Me: Did the first time out meet your expectations?

Trump: It far exceeded them. I had no idea this tournament would be as important as it turned out. I thought we would have a nice tournament, that we would have some of the big pros. But I had no idea we'd get this kind of tournament, with all the press coverage, the magnitude of the players.

Me: Steve Wynn is coming to Atlantic City. Any chance of Donald Trump going to Las Vegas?

Trump: Yes, I think I will go to Las Vegas. Las Vegas is having a little rough time now, as you know, and I think I will go there. The Trump Taj Mahal is number one in Atlantic City and the Trump Plaza is number two. There seems to be not much more I can do to eclipse myself in Atlantic City. It's hard to be number one and number two. Very difficult, because you have a certain detraction. You're competing against yourself. So that number one and number two is amazing. We want to continue to do great with these places, but yes, I will be going to Las Vegas, perhaps in the not-too-distant future. The company is geared up to do whatever we want to do there.

The camera crew is ready. The gorgeous reporter is striding toward Donald, her short black skirt doing exactly what a short black skirt is supposed to do. My interview with Trump is most definitely over.

* * *

Fierce play during Day Two finally eliminates the Girl from Baywatch from the proceedings. "You mean I don't

190

get to keep any of my money?" she jokes, making an exceedingly graceful exit from the felt-covered battleground. Astoundingly, Ms. Bleeth comes in 29th place, outlasting five World Champions and dozens of other grizzled poker veterans and perennial contenders.

Among the remaining hopefuls are young Ted Forrest, who recently won three World Series titles in one year; Dr. Bruce Van Horn, the 1996 runner-up in the World Series championship event; and Kassem "Freddie" Deeb, a regular in the Mirage's "biggest game in town." It's an exceptionally strong field, with big-name players at every table. Cyndy Violette and Phil Hellmuth still have chips, as do World Series titleists Tom McEvoy, Frank Henderson, and Noli Francisco. And so does one William McKinney, 72, from Kingsport, Tennessee, whose grandson watches proudly as Grandpappy chews on an unlit stogie, chats with his youthful competition, and somehow manages to bob and weave, fold and raise, until he's made it to the final table. It's his second poker tournament ever.

Yes, poker dreams sometimes do come true. At the United States Poker Championship, two Vietnamese immigrants, Nhut Tran and Men Nguyen, finish 1-2 in the Best All-Around Player competition, tabulated over the course of 21 preliminary events, and respectively earn $30,000 and $20,000 bonuses. When Tran and Nguyen talk about America as the land of opportunity, they mean it.

But by the end of Day Two, most of the players—and their poker dreams—have been extinguished. Only six contestants remain, chief among them Mr. Hellmuth, who has built what should be an insurmountable chip lead. He has $207,000. His closest opponent has $138,500.

But funny things can happen when you're playing for $500,000 under the hot television lights, with hundreds of spectators (including the guy who owns the casino) watching your every twitch. Hellmuth begins Day Three playing his typical game, steamrolling anyone who dares to challenge him. After a string of "bad beats" (unluckily losing hands when he is the odds-on mathematical favorite),

Hellmuth goes "on tilt," as gamblers say, and begins playing poker with his boiling emotions, not his cool head. This is not the recommended method for winning a major championship, whether you're a master of the game or a nymph from "Baywatch." Hellmuth does not last. Late in the day, Ken Flaton, from Henderson, Nevada, sends the former World Champ packing. Shortly thereafter, Flaton eliminates Surinder Sunar, from Wolverhampton, England, and earns the title of United States Poker Champion.

Elated by his victory, Flaton tells me he grew up in North Bergen, New Jersey, and worked briefly as a vendor at Madison Square Garden, where he sold peanuts and popcorn. After a brief career as an accountant and bookkeeper, he took up poker professionally. That was 22 years ago.

"I'm very proud to have won this championship in its first year," Flaton says. "That's like becoming part of history. I'm going to look forward to coming back here next year as the defending champ. Something tells me," Flaton says, smiling wryly in Donald Trump's direction, "that next year is going to be even bigger and better."

22

The Grand Old Man

Johnny Moss, one of the greatest poker players to have ever played the game, is dead.

To call him legendary would be a gross understatement, like calling Frank Sinatra a good singer. Moss was known as the "Grand Old Man" of poker, one of the seminal figures in the storied history of America's favorite indoor game. He was one of only two players to have won the World Series of Poker World Championship three times. (Alas, if the annual competition at Binion's Horseshoe had begun decades earlier, before Moss began to feel the ravages of age, there's no telling how many titles he might have captured.) He was renowned for breaking Nick "the Greek" Dandolos in a famous marathon game of five-card stud. The history books do not agree on how much the Grand Old Man took from the Greek, but Moss himself recalled the figure being close to $4 million. He played with virtually everyone of note in the annals of 20th-century poker, from celebrated World Champions to secretive road gamblers, with name-brand millionaires and anonymous scrabblers. Even when players knew they had little hope of beating the man, many gambled with him anyway, just to say they had lost to the best. All poker waters in our time flowed through Johnny Moss.

"Johnny's passing is the end of an era," Jim Albrecht,

the World Series of Poker tournament director, said recently. "He was the link between the Old West school of gambling and the modern days of a forty-page rule book. Ask all the living legends, they'll all credit Johnny Moss with being the last of the great road gamblers. He was the Master. And now the Master is gone."

Doyle Brunson, Johnny Moss' longtime friend and colleague, said, "In his time Johnny Moss was the dominant player in the game. Nobody had more devotion to poker, and nobody played more. He probably put in more hours at the table than anyone in history. If anybody had an influence on me as a poker player, it was Johnny. I learned everything I know from watching him and playing at the same table."

Of all his thousands of Johnny Moss anecdotes and memories, Doyle Brunson said the thing he'll always remember most about his mentor is this: "Johnny always said, 'A gambler lives like a millionaire whether he is or he isn't.' I think Johnny Moss proved that statement better than anyone."

If you were to have encountered Johnny Moss outside his natural element, away from the milieu in which he normally operated, he might have struck you as a harmless slightly dotty old man. Put him on a park bench surrounded by pigeons and screaming toddlers and you would have thought him a nattily attired gentleman watching the world go by, stretching his pension into the twilight of his years. Unless you looked closely, nothing would have indicated that this elderly retiree was anything but an elderly retiree, benignly passing his days on the outskirts of life.

Look into his eyes, though, and you might have been startled. Near the end they were tired and dewy, as befits a man of 88. But those eyes were piercing, too. Hooded like an alligator's, they regarded the world with a cold intensity that was simultaneously inspiring and chilling.

Johnny Moss had eyes that had seen things most of us believe happen only in movies, or tales of fantasy. His eyes detected a faint pulse of apprehension in the veins of a man's

194

neck facing a crucial decision. They saw delicate acts of leg-erdemain and brutal acts of violence. Johnny Moss wit-nessed men losing millions of dollars on the turn of a card.

Fittingly, Mr. Moss held court virtually every day of the week at Binion's Horseshoe in downtown Las Vegas. You could usually find him at the $20-$40 hold 'em game or entered in a major tournament. By the luck of the draw, a rank beginner might have found himself and his pile of chips seated across from Moss at one of these tournaments, vaguely aware that after a few hours all he'd likely have to show for his efforts would be a pile of memories. But he was thrilled anyway. It was like playing in a pro-am with Jack Nicklaus.

Everyone has a favorite Johnny Moss story, most of which involve winning a meager pot from the old master, or perhaps learning a money-saving lesson from the reptil-ian-eyed man who had lived through about all there has ever been to experience at a poker table. In fact, with a mix-ture of pride and chagrin, I recall being knocked out of my first World Series of Poker many years ago by Johnny Moss, whose pair of kings sent a young reporter and his scruffy pair of jacks packing. (Strangely, losing the tournament felt somehow honorable at that moment.) A year later, incre-mentally wiser, I enjoyed one of the highlights of my poker life when I knocked Mr. Moss out of the World Series seven-card stud event, thereby joining the voluminous list of ama-teur poker players who will one day tell anyone who'll lis-ten that they once competed against the great Johnny Moss—and beat him out of a pot!

To see Moss at the end of his life, nearly 90, was akin to watching a punchy Muhammad Ali sign autographs at a baseball-card convention. Debilitated by ill health, Johnny Moss got around on a motorized electric cart, whose horn he seemed to delight in honking as he wound through ca-sino traffic. He spoke in a hoarse Texas-inflected whisper, and his thoughts often strayed randomly, making extended conversation difficult. His memory was no longer reliable. In 1995, for the first time since the World Series of Poker's inception in 1970—he was its first winner—Johnny Moss did not enter the World Championship, primarily because of fatigue.

He was a frail old man. But something magical happened when Johnny Moss parked his little cart next to a poker table. The senility disappeared. The aches and pains diminished. The eyes burned bright. Like the severely retarded boy who plays Chopin nocturnes on his mom's piano or the autistic man who paints photo-realistic landscapes from memory, Johnny Moss experienced a curious rebirth every time he played cards. Whether sheerly through professional prowess or acute instincts, the Grand Old Man, at 88, remained a winning poker player.

In his last interview, which he granted several weeks before his death, he told me, "I been playing since I was ten years old." Surveying the Horseshoe's expansive poker room, humming with the clatter of chips and the riffling of cards, Moss chuckled. "I guess I know what I'm doing by now."

As a boy in Odessa, Texas, Johnny Moss said he was "learned by a gang of cheaters," who introduced him to the joys of chicanery, showing him the secrets of dealing from the bottom of the deck, holding out cards, and introducing marked decks into high-stakes games. "They taught me how to cheat," Moss recalled. "But they taught me how to protect myself, too." As a teenager Moss procured a job at a local saloon, where he was responsible for cleaning up a dirty game. "I made ten to twenty dollars a day for two years, just watching the game, keeping an eye on everything." It was during this intensive observational period that Moss first learned the finer points of poker.

"After I picked up a thing or two, I became a road gambler, playing on the square wherever I could find a good game. Mexico. Tahoe. Wherever. I knew how to do it, but didn't have to steal. I made plenty playing clean. But I sure saw a lot of cheating in those days," Moss reported. "One night I'm playing in some small town—I don't remember where, maybe in Oklahoma—and I see they got the room set up as a peep joint [with a confederate spying on players' cards through a peek hole in the ceiling]. So I pull out my gun—always carried a gun back in those days—and said, 'Now, fellas, do I have to go and shoot a bullet in the ceiling? Or you going to send your boy down without any harm?' Hell, they thought I was bluffing," Moss laughed. "Ended up shooting the guy in his ass."

Back when the gambling world was run by bootleggers and mobsters, before publicly traded corporations cornered the market on suckers, Johnny Moss said being a professional gambler was truly like living on the wild frontier, where pointing a pistol at a man's forehead and ordering him to undress was not a particularly unusual request. "I suppose I found about fifteen hold-out machines [mechanical cheating devices] on naked men through the years."

Did he ever kill a man?

"I don't know if he died," Moss said.

In one legendary gambling story, Moss was playing golf against a wealthy businessman, offering the mark his standard proposition: Moss would play from the back tees; his opponent would automatically begin each hole on the green in regulation, playing from a spot on the putting surface of Johnny's choosing. "I was so good from the fairway I always got inside of them on my approach shot. I made millions on that golf bet," Moss crowed. But one day, in Las Vegas, the blind hog had found the acorn, as gamblers (and golfers) like to say: The sucker had the hustler on the run. "I think I was down about a quarter-million going into the last few holes," Moss recalled. "Fact was, the *other* guy was in trouble." Serious trouble. Johnny's backers happened to be a couple of unsavory types who advocated simply killing Moss' opponent rather than paying him off. "I made birdie on the last hole. Cost the guy about one-hundred thousand dollars. He was complaining and hollering. He said to me, 'Moss, you're the luckiest man alive.' I said, 'No, sir, you are.' He had no idea my birdie probably saved his life.

"Sure, I had plenty of mob connections through the

197

years," Moss admitted. "Some of them weren't bad. Hell, I lived in Bugsy's place at the Flamingo for three or four years," he claimed.

Johnny Moss' greatest benefactor, however, was his best friend from childhood, Benny Binion, who after a lucrative career in the Dallas moonshine and gambling rackets, moved to Las Vegas in the '40s after his sheriff got beat in an election. It was Binion, an illiterate, self-taught, financial genius, who arranged the storied match between Moss and Nick the Greek. In 1949, the Greek, wowing Vegas with his extravagant wagers, told Benny Binion he was looking for someone to play poker with, someone who might fancy a $250,000 no-limit contest. Binion thought Johnny Moss was the best poker player in the world, perhaps the only man fit to gamble with Dandolos for what was then a monumental sum.

"Johnny, I got this game all set up for you," Binion told Moss. "What do you want to do?"

"Leave town," Moss replied.

He didn't. Benny Binion, figuring the match would do for his business what exploding volcanoes and pirate ship battles have done for Steve Wynn, convinced Moss to play the match. Close to five months, thousands of hands, and millions of dollars later, Dandolos conceded. "Mr. Moss," the Greek said, "I must let you go."

"That Greek was always a gentleman," Moss remembered.

Seated at a crowded poker table, raking in several magnificent pots as if on cue, as if he intended to impress nearby observers with his still-potent skills, Johnny Moss scanned the casino floor. His head turned slowly, watching an elderly lady pumping coins into a slot machine; a young couple at the blackjack table; a drunk digging in his pockets for another quarter. "It's pitiful the shape people get in," Moss said. "But I never felt sorry for the losers."

Johnny Moss admitted to having had a "leak" at the gaming tables, a compulsion to blow all the money he earned playing poker and golf and bowling—"I won over two million at the bowling alley," he claimed—on sports betting and craps. "In four years I lost over eight million at the dice tables, betting football, playing three-hundred-thousand dollars on the middles [long-shot sports wagering]. One day I'd be giving my wife two-hundred thousand, tell her to go buy a house. Pick out whatever you want. Next day I'd be going broke, asking her to have the money returned." Eventually Moss quit the dice and the sports and the cigarettes. "My eyesight suddenly got better. My bankroll got better, too. I guess I been all right ever since," he said, smiling slyly.

He won another pot, a huge one, with a flush. His opponents watched disconsolately as what was once their horde of chips formed a sizable heap in front of the elderly fellow with the little cap and the lizard eyes. "Nice hand, Mr. Moss," one of the losers said. "Very nice."

Johnny Moss allowed himself a subdued laugh. "I been a sucker now for seventy, eighty years. Long, long time." He stacked his winnings into neat hundred-dollar towers. "Not bad for a sucker. No, not too bad."

23

The Mozart of the
Poker Table

A jostling crowd of spectators gathers around the poker table, peeking over shoulders and around chairs, stepping on toes and bumping into neighbors—all to get a glimpse of some guys playing a game of cards.

Were the site anywhere but Binion's Horseshoe Hotel and Casino in downtown Las Vegas, home of the World Series of Poker, the commotion might be hard to fathom. But the participants at this particular game of cards are competing for more than $150,000 in cash, the first-place prize money for the no-limit Texas hold 'em event at the prestigious Hall of Fame Poker Classic. Moreover, one of the players is Phil Hellmuth Jr.

If poker tournaments were entertainment events to which promoters could sell admission tickets, Hellmuth would easily be the hottest draw. He's magnetic, entertaining, and controversial. And he is oftentimes spectacular, displaying tournament poker skills that suggest innate genius. He is, in the view of many, the greatest tournament poker player in the world.

In a universe where diamond rings and gold chains seem like compulsory accessories, where stacks of $100 bills are tossed about like so much Monopoly money, where power and ruthlessness and trickery are considered necessary attributes, Hellmuth stands out from the majority of poker professionals like an Eagle Scout among hardened criminals. Close to 6 feet 6 inches tall, with a complexion that has never quite recovered from adolescent acne and a smile that, not long ago, hid a full set of braces, Hellmuth barely looks his 34 years. To the uninitiated, he would seem better off back where he grew up, in Madison, Wisconsin, playing video games and pickup basketball rather than vying for piles of cash against sharpies from Texas and Nevada.

Of course, if you've ever seen Phil Hellmuth at the final table of one of the Horseshoe's major tournaments—a spot he occupies with impressive frequency—you know he belongs in this milieu. He's the son of an assistant dean of the College of Letters and Science at the University of Wisconsin, yet his metier is not in the world of scholastics but of money-laden tables and steely-eyed gamblers.

In 1989, at the remarkable age of 24, Hellmuth won the poker championship of the world, serving notice that a brash kid from America's Dairyland was one of the most devastating players in the brief history of high-stakes poker tournaments. Hellmuth instantly became a household name among serious players everywhere.

He was considered a prodigy, a Mozart of the cards who dared to tangle with the big boys—and beat them. His was one of the most compelling, and unlikely, success stories to happen in a city where an underdog winning against overwhelming odds is a favorite myth.

Hellmuth made the myth come true.

And then he lost it. Arrogant, snide, insulting—the epitome of a poor winner—the Madison boy-wonder flaunted his triumphs in the face of his competitors. When he lost a pot to someone he considered an inferior player, he would berate his opponent mercilessly and challenge him to play heads-up. When he lost a tournament, he would storm out of Binion's card-table arena and slam a few chairs around his hotel room.

He was widely disliked. In some quarters he still is.

"Having such big success so early, I thought I was some

sort of poker god," Hellmuth says, sipping, as a good Wisconsin boy ought to, a glass of milk in the Horseshoe buffet. Phil has recently made another in-the-money showing at the Hall of Fame, and, naturally, he's elated. But he's not giddy with the trademark braggadocio people have come to expect of him. Indeed, he sounds almost contrite. "I was telling people I was the best," he says of the time following his record-setting World Series victory. "I was sure I was the best. I guess my ego got out of line."

Knowing something about his life before poker, it's easy to see how Hellmuth became the John McEnroe of the cardroom, a cocky brat with undeniable talent who managed to rub just about everyone the wrong way. In high school at Madison West, he never applied himself and, he admits, earned "bad grades." Fiercely competitive and virtually friendless, Hellmuth soothed himself by cultivating what he calls "a massive ego." Lacking both a satisfying social life and any clearly defined goals, he was a lonely underachiever, a gangly outsider who, despite any tangible achievements, always sensed he would do something great. "I didn't know what it would be or when it would happen, but I knew," Hellmuth says. "I knew someday..." He grins as he remembers. But his turquoise eyes are dewy, and they burn with a startling intensity.

Thanks to one successful semester of high school (and, he confesses, his father's academic standing), Hellmuth was accepted into the University of Wisconsin as a special-admission student. He thought college might be a place where he could blossom, where the potential locked within him would be unleashed. He even planned on attending the university's School of Business.

"I come from a liberal middle-class background," he says. "I wanted to make my family proud."

But Hellmuth's freshman year was turned nightmarish by a terrible case of warts, which blanketed his hands, and an outbreak of acne, which covered his boyish face with pimples. He was the butt of practical jokes. Some dormmates, for instance, "nominated" Phil for dorm president and talked the lanky lad into making a speech for an election that, it turned out, had already been determined. As the months passed, he drifted increasingly closer to the margins of collegiate life. In his sophomore year Hellmuth tried some recreational drugs; they held little interest. In his junior year he tried poker; he was addicted.

A friend took him to Memorial Union, where a group of professors and Madison-area professionals played an ongoing game of no-limit hold 'em. "These guys were using Austrian coins, dimes, for chips. And it didn't look like you could lose much, so I sat down and played," Hellmuth recalls. "I lost twenty dollars that first night, which back then was a lot of money. I hadn't even paid my tuition at that point, so it hurt. The next time I went I lost thirty dollars. Now I'm down fifty, which I really can't afford to lose. I had no money; I was eating dinner at home. But the next time I played I won four-hundred-fifty dollars."

Hellmuth paid his tuition with his winnings, only to quickly fall behind in his classes and drop out. He worked for minimum wage hoeing and pulling weeds in a farmer's field and used the money to play poker, where, after a month and a half, he won enough to quit his job.

Gradually, as his ability grew to match his aspirations, Hellmuth began to win consistently—and big. "I started to play in larger games, taking home over one thousand a night. I didn't really have any idea how good I was; I just enjoyed playing."

After beating a group of Madison doctors and lawyers for $2,700, he re-enrolled in school. Soon, though, he dropped out for good. "I never did well in school," Hellmuth recalls. "I didn't care enough. I just cared about poker."

With his success came the confidence needed to take on the professionals in Las Vegas. At Binion's, Hellmuth devoted two years to his graduate degree in poker, a roller-coaster ride of success and failure. In 1989, Hellmuth squared off against two-time titleholder Johnny Chan at the Horseshoe's final table—and walked away as the new world champion of poker.

About the only person who wasn't shocked was Phil Hellmuth Jr. He knew he had a special gift.

"Sometimes," he says, "I get very good reads on what people are thinking or doing. Especially when they show emotion. When there's a hundred-thousand dollars on the line, players tend to get nervous. And I can read them."

Doesn't he, too, get jittery at those stakes? "Sure," Hellmuth replies, "but instead I try to concentrate on the basics."

He bought his dad a Mercedes-Benz, contributed generously to the university, aided his siblings with their college funds, and treated himself to a midnight-blue Porsche and a Lake Mendota condominium—and spent the rest of his big bankroll in less than a year. But gone with the money were also his swaggering self-confidence and his winning performances. Not only did Hellmuth lose his coveted title at the next World Series, he didn't even place in the top 50. And in a handful of smaller tournaments he never managed to finish in the money.

"I thought I was unbeatable, that I should never lose. But I was losing," he says, staring off into a bank of clattering slot machines. "I hated myself for not playing great. I'd ask myself, 'Why are you playing so bad? Why can't you control it?' I suffered from a lot of self-imposed pressure."

The veteran players who had watched Hellmuth ascend so quickly were overjoyed to watch him fall. The ill will he generated early in his career persists to this day. While a handful of friends—mostly comrades from Wisconsin—speak well of Phil Hellmuth, the professional poker players at Binion's Horseshoe, one after another, have nothing nice to say about the youthful champion.

"He's the luckiest son of a bitch I've ever seen."

"He can't play worth shit."

"He's an egomaniac."

He's "aggravating," "irritating," "annoying." Interestingly, though, not one of Hellmuth's critics was willing to make his evaluation for attribution. While they may dislike him personally or profess to disrespect him professionally, the majority of tournament poker players still hate finding themselves at the same table as "the Kid." For a player thought of, by some at least, as a "lucky jerk," he's among the most feared competitors in the business.

One pro willing to speak his mind without the shield of anonymity is former world champ "Amarillo Slim" Preston, the charismatic Texan whose garrulous style has made him one of the most recognized poker players in the world. "There's absolutely nothing wrong with that boy," Slim says of Hellmuth. "He just needs a little fixin', that's all."

Despite the periodic downturns in Phil Hellmuth's fortunes, he's refused to slink off into oblivion; he's refused to be an intriguing footnote to poker lore. Instead, he's decided to "do a little fixin'."

* * *

Hellmuth, now 34, has done a lot of growing up. Marriage, he says, has mellowed him. Family life, he says, beaming, is "just fantastic." His two sons, Philip III, 8, and Nicholas, 5, and his wife Kathy, a psychiatrist doing her residency at Stanford, have helped him to see there's more to life than gambling. "This game used to be number one. Now it's my family. I guess being a husband and father has given me a sense of contentment, which makes it easier to be gracious in victory and defeat. What it all comes down to is you've got to like yourself. You've got to be comfortable with yourself. And having a family has helped me realize I'm a good guy. I've gone through a lot. But the struggle has always made me better."

His opponents, he says, had better watch out. Hellmuth is better than ever. "I'm over my ego problems now, I'm happy with myself, and everything is starting to click. When it does, I play really well. All the people who don't respect my play—they're in trouble. I'm going to bust them."

For a moment, Hellmuth sounds as if he's full of his old bluster. But the conviction and matter-of-factness with which he proclaims that he will surprise a lot of doubters—

that, in fact, he will recapture the world championship—make you feel as if he is simply telling the truth.

And if you don't believe him, those piercing eyes seem to imply, just watch.

Historically, Hellmuth goes on significant tears, wild hot (and cold) streaks that cannot be explained adequately by standard statistical analysis. In 1991 he finished in the top five in four Hall of Fame events. In '93 he won three World Series events; and in the 1994 Hall of Fame Championship he won the main event. But for every upswing in his fortunes there have been some precipitous downturns as well. One noted pro told me that when Hellmuth is playing well he's virtually unbeatable, easily the best tournament poker player on earth. But when he's off his game, "Phil stinks. I mean he's *really* bad. You never know which Phil is going to show up."

Another famous pro, who has faced Phil at numerous final tables, says, "Phil Hellmuth can be the player you would least like to face heads-up or the one you would most like to face. I've seen him make plays that were horrible, borderline amateur, like you would expect from someone who has barely ever played before. And other times the guy is brilliant. Untouchable. He makes you wonder how anyone can be that good."

Those who have tangled with Phil Hellmuth in the large side games that spring up around the tournament action profess little surprise at Hellmuth's performance. "He'll tell you he kills the live games," one professional side-game player says. "But the fact is, he just goes up and down. One session he'll make a killing and the next one he'll give it all back. I don't think he has the patience to be a good live-game player. Too anxious to break everybody. Too inconsistent."

Hellmuth acknowledges his dual nature. "I've had to struggle to learn to play *consistently* great," Hellmuth says, horsing around with his two boys in his suburban Menlo Park, California, home. "I think achieving greatness so early on was hard on me, especially since I had such low self-esteem. You put those two things together and it's a bad combination."

Another factor in Phil Hellmuth's on-fire/ice-cold duality has been, he admits, a disastrous foray into the investing business—investing in other tournament players. "I'll be honest: I lost a lot of money backing people," Hellmuth says, bouncing his son "Niko" on his knee. "I don't think I won a major tournament the entire time I was backing other players. It was just a big distraction. I ended up worrying about my investments, not myself."

In fact, the first occasion in which Hellmuth had no "horses" and retained a full percentage of his winnings— he had previously traded off percentage points with other top players—he won the limit hold 'em tournament at the Hall of Fame.

Another source of Hellmuth's dialectical performance may be his penchant for loony proposition bets. In 1994 he laid 8-5 that he would win a World Series event; in 1995 Hellmuth bet one top pro $10,000 at even odds that he'd win an event. "I admit those bets can be a little distracting," Hellmuth says. "But I'll continue to make them if they're profitable."

Does his predilection for proposition bets indicate a compulsive character, a thirst for action, no matter the costs? "I'm *not* compulsive," Hellmuth says, smiling. The prop bets, he insists, are fun, entertaining diversions, and in the grand scheme of his financial well-being, relatively small. Hellmuth's computer versus his pal Huck Seed for $500 a point at Chinese poker? Nine-ball at $2,000 a game? Thousands of dollars on sinking a three-pointer on the basketball court? Bets on backgammon, ice skating, and, yes, *pinball?* "Strictly entertainment," Hellmuth says, shrugging.

His wife, he says, hates the prop bets. "She wants me just to play poker. But I don't really make that many bets. And before I do I study the bet, so it becomes more a bet of skill, not luck. And if I do bet, it's not for much," Hellmuth says. For example, when he makes the rare sports bet it's seldom for more than $1,000. "And if it's a poker proposition I definitely feel like I'm getting the best of it."

Aside from poker, Phil Hellmuth's most compelling gambling passion is golf. He plays often—and for stakes that would cripple the average hacker's bankroll. "I'll play a two-thousand-dollar Nassau. It's extremely fun when you have to make a putt that's worth six-thousand dollars. You feel like a pro," Hellmuth explains. Golf, like poker, according to Hellmuth, is all about handling pressure. "I like to rise to the challenge, to see how I react to the pressure putts. And you know what? I tend to make a lot of them."

When not jetting off to play golf with his high-rolling buddies, Phil Hellmuth is an enthusiastic, unabashed family man. Seeing him playing tag or horsey or power rangers with his two boys is to witness a profoundly content father.

But some in the poker community have questioned why a devout committed father, a vital *provider*, should allow himself legendary—some would say profligate—shopping sprees at places like the Forum Shops at Caesars Palace. "I assume those people are talking about the shirt." Indeed, Hellmuth caused something of a stir when he showed up at the 1995 Four Queens tournament in a $1,700 silk shirt adorned with stylized honey bees.

"Look, I bought that shirt specifically to win the tournament," he explains. "It made me feel good; it was dazzling. I knew that if I bought it I would win. And, just like I predicted, I did. If people had a comment about my shopping at the time, I don't think they do anymore."

Hellmuth currently favors Versace. "Ever since I started wearing these clothes, I've been winning. They pay for themselves."

Recently a rumor circulated through the tournament-poker community that Phil Hellmuth Jr. was, for all intents and purposes, broke. The player-backing, and the prop bets, and the inconsistent play had finally caught up with him, the story went. The prodigy was a few dollars away from the rail.

"Not really true," Hellmuth says calmly. "I wasn't broke. I was almost out of my bankroll money, but I had plenty left over for my family and our expenses. This kind of situation occurs sometimes when you have the kind of lifestyle I lead. But you've got to understand something..."

Phil Hellmuth stares at me intently, measuring his words. "I don't have any worries. I am the best tournament poker player in the world. If I need to do something, I'll do it."

On the eve of a major tournament at Binion's, Phil's wife Kathy called to tell him that, as far as she could figure, their finances weren't looking too well. She offered to lessen the monthly budget by cutting back on non-essential expenses; she suggested canceling her car-phone service. Phil told her not to. And then he promptly went on to earn nearly a quarter-million dollars at the poker table. (The phone remained in service.)

"Other people have more concern for me than I do," Hellmuth believes. "Whenever I'm confronted by need I respond. When 'need' comes in, 'perfect' comes out the other end."

Phil Hellmuth Jr. has been playing a lot of perfect poker lately. As he's demonstrated numerous times in the past decade, when he's playing his "A" game, Hellmuth is a frighteningly effective competitor. In fact, not only is Phil poised to overtake Johnny Chan as the all-time leading money winner at the World Series of Poker, he remains one of the only players in history to amass more than $1 million in earnings *exclusive of the main event.* "That amount will get bigger, too," Hellmuth says matter-of-factly. "I can guarantee I'm going to win an event at this World Series. I'm playing too well not to."

Phil Hellmuth's visibility—and marketability—in the poker world has grown in step with his record-setting winnings. In fact, Hellmuth is one of the few professional tournament-poker players to have a sponsorship deal. Bay 101, Phil's neighborhood cardroom, pays him $1,000 a week to play in its Sunday hold 'em tournament, and to wear a Bay 101 hat when he sits down at a major tournament and when he poses with his winnings.

Lately that's been often. When he's at his best he tends to talk less at the poker table, relying more on his ability to read an opponent than to intimidate him with verbal barbs. He plays aggressively, threateningly, dangerously.

When he makes a substantial bet—say, $50,000 or more—at a tournament final table, and his opponent is considering calling, Hellmuth freezes, as if momentarily caught in a science-fiction-villain's ray-gun. He's nearly impossible to figure.

Only Kathy Hellmuth claims to know when her husband is bluffing. The competition can only guess—and pray they're right. Anyone trying to determine the strength of Phil's cards lacks the benefit of watching his motions, which might otherwise betray his hand. The annoying intimidating chatterer suddenly turns to stone.

Except for one thing. Hellmuth's eyes are alive. Though they, too, are still, you can tell they're focused and alert, seeing everything on the periphery without shifting from their locked-straight-ahead position. To the hundreds of spectators gathered at the leather rail, craning to get a peek at the hundreds of thousands of dollars piled on the green-baize table, Hellmuth appears to be staring at something in the distance. Something calling to him. Something that sends him far away from the tension and the pressure and the hysteria of betting a middle-class-American's yearly salary on a single hand of poker. He seems profoundly peaceful.

As his opponent frets, studying the cards, the pot of $1,000 chips, the crowd, Hellmuth gazes across the room to the far wall, past the onlookers, past the side games, past the commotion. He might claim he's looking at a light bulb or an empty chair.

But to the crowd gathered around the best tournament poker player on the planet, Phil Hellmuth seems to be staring at Binion's Poker Hall of Fame, intently studying the photographed faces of the immortal players enshrined there, never losing sight of the empty available spaces beside them.

24

The Adventures of Huckleberry Seed

His name is Huck Seed.

When your name is Huck Seed, most people expect you to be a pig farmer. They expect you to come to a big shiny city like Las Vegas and get all goggle-eyed and dumbstruck, like Gomer Pyle. "Gaaawwly! Them are some big ol' buildings!" With a name like Huck Seed, you get used to hardened Las Vegas gamblers figuring that you stumbled into town falling off the back of a turnip truck.

When your name is Huck Seed *and* you're 27 years old, sort of shy, and a bit of a loner—well, it's easy to understand why some cynical types might not take you seriously, how people might underestimate you.

It's easy to see why people who have been around gambling for a long time might have difficulty imagining the phrase "Huck Seed, World Champion of Poker."

I mean, come on, your name after all is *Huck Seed.*

But that's the great thing about playing cards: They don't care what you look like, or how old you are, or whether you're a boy or girl. And they certainly don't give a damn what your name is.

No, the game of poker rewards the man who plays his cards best. Doesn't matter where you've come from; doesn't matter where you're going. Doesn't matter if you wear diamond pinkie rings or dress in T-shirts and sweats. Doesn't matter if your dad is the mayor of Chicago or the dog-catcher of North Platte, Nebraska. All that matters is how you play your cards.

And at the 1996 World Series of Poker in downtown Las Vegas, the man who did that best was a young loner named Huck Seed.

He defeated 294 of the greatest poker players on earth, all of whom put up $10,000 to enter the no-limit hold 'em championship event at Binion's Horseshoe casino. At the start of the tournament, every player had $10,000 in chips stacked in front of him. After four days of competition, all the chips were stacked in front of Huck Seed. For his accomplishment, the enigmatic gambler was awarded the title World Champion of Poker, a 14-karat-gold commemorative bracelet, and some prize money.

One million dollars, to be exact.

All of a sudden, the world wanted to know: Who is this guy?

Huck Seed wasn't saying. His official bio, the one Binion's Horseshoe distributed to the press before the beginning of the final round of action, was only five lines long. It said, in part, "Huck Seed, a 27-year-old professional poker player from Las Vegas, has finished in the money in numerous major poker competitions. This is his first time to cash in the championship tournament." Later, reporters discovered that the young Mr. Seed had been enrolled at Cal Tech, the MIT of the west coast, where he studied electrical engineering. (There was a rumor going around—later denied—that he'd developed some kind of sophisticated computer program to teach himself to win at cards.) After taking a leave of absence in 1989, he started playing poker and never returned to college.

That was it. That was all Huck Seed would tell. He seemed to be suggesting, what you need to know you can see: young handsome man; single, with a knockout girl-friend; very accomplished poker player; millionaire. Any more questions?

Sure, Huck. For instance, how does a college drop-out

become good enough to win the World Series of Poker? What's it like to be 27 and known as the best poker player in the world? And, what's with the name?

* * *

Huck Seed has a reputation for aggression. When he enters a pot he's usually raising, making nine other guys guess, making everyone wonder, does he have it? Or is he bluffing? Huck makes it expensive to find out.

Late in the tournament, with only 40 players left, Huck, acting last, makes a large raise. He bets $100,000. Sensing the young loner might be "on the steal," Tom Jacobs, a perennial contender from Colorado, calls the bet. Including the antes, there's close to a quarter-million dollars in the pot.

* * *

Huck Seed remains something of a mystery. Shortly after his World Series triumph, my repeated attempts to reach the reclusive World Champion were unsuccessful. He was supposedly traveling in Europe, competing in a backgammon tournament. (Huck is a world-class competitor in that game as well.) This much is certain: Poker has never had a potentially better ambassador for the game who has possessed less interest in being an ambassador for the game. Huck Seed just wants to play cards, win money, and blend into the neon lights. He's a reluctant superstar.

"I don't know how I feel about being called the world champion of poker," Seed said to me, shortly after winning the $1 million title. "I know I can play really well, and I expected to win. I was pretty confident." But, he added, he never dreamed he'd be the world champion of anything. To him, being the best poker player on earth is not about a title; it's about being a winner.

* * *

The dealer turns the flop: 2, 4, 6, of various suits. Tom, act-ing first, bets $200,000. Huck does not react. He stares blankly at his opponent, then at the pot, then back at his opponent, sizing him up. Betraying not even a flicker of emotion, Huck says, "Raise," and pushes all his chips—about $400,000—toward the center of the pot. Tom, after much deliberation, decides to call. There is well over $1 million in the pot.

Both players turn over their hole cards. Huck has a 5-6, giv-ing him a pair of sixes. Tom is holding a pair of sevens, the better hand. If the dealer turns two blanks, Tom will win the pot and Huck will be out of the tournament. He knows he's a huge un-derdog at this point, but Huck does not react.

The next card is a queen. Tom is still winning. There are only nine cards in the deck that can save young Huck Seed now: the straight-filling 3s, the three remaining 5s, and the two re-maining 6s. Huck's face does not change expression.

The dealer turns the final card. It's a six.

He pulls in $1 million in chips. And he does not react.

* * *

Huck Seed grew up in Montana, where his dad, a writer and poker player, had a job producing pamphlets for the state. According to Seed's close friend, Phil Hellmuth Jr., everyone in the middle-class Seed family was brilliant—brilliant enough to earn scholarships to places like Cal Tech. "He was like me," Hellmuth recalls. "He started making more money playing poker than he ever would from a col-lege education, so he dropped out and hit the big time."

Hellmuth thinks the similarities between him and Seed do not stop there. "In so many ways he reminds me of my-self. Both of us came from modest backgrounds. We both rose up quickly and we both developed big egos."

Huck, the quiet country boy? A big ego?

"Oh, sure," Hellmuth says, laughing. "Once we were playing a short-handed game, a three-person table, and I was winning all the money. I must of been winning close to a hundred thousand [dollars] in about two days. Lots of it from Huck. So Huck says to me, 'Phil, I'm losing a little bit to you now, but I've busted better players than you.' It was the kind of brash thing I would have said when I was younger."

Hellmuth thinks Seed's personality is the product of a lethal combination: youth and talent. "Huck's talent at poker showed real early," the former World Champ recalls. "At age twenty-two he won a million-two in ten days playing no-limit with two of the biggest gamblers in the world. That kind of score will give you confidence."

* * *

Later in the tournament, with only four players remaining, one of whom will be crowned World Champion of Poker, Huck makes another bold play. He has raised eight out of the last 10 pots. Some experts think he's "on tilt," emotionally off-kilter. They think Huck Seed is "steaming." Others believe he's simply playing the aggressive, enigmatic game that is his trademark. His three opponents, however, do not care why Huck is raising like a madman; they just want the young aggressor to stop stealing their chips.

* * *

How does a 22-year-old find himself playing the world's biggest gamblers for those kinds of stakes? How does he build a bankroll big enough to play in such a heady game? In Huck Seed's case, his initial rise to poker stardom came in the $50- and $100-limit games in card clubs around San Jose, where he consistently beat the local Silicon Valley heavyweights for thousands of dollars. Then, according to Hellmuth, Huck's big financial break came in 1991, when he wisely invested in a 40% stake in Brad Daugherty, who went on to become that year's $1 million champion. With his now bulging bankroll, Huck Seed went back to California and played in the biggest games Los Angeles had to offer, $300-$600 and $400-$800 limits. One Hollywood "agent to the stars" lost millions in those games, and Seed was one of the fortunate recipients. He was now a very wealthy young man.

There were, of course, losses, too, times when Huck Seed was nearly broke. But, Phil Hellmuth explains, "Huck's never been flat broke. He's been close. But it's never really happened to him. He's never been completely down and out. So he knows no fear. That's his big advantage. He knows no fear."

Every professional poker player you talk to says the same thing about Huck Seed's poker-playing abilities: "He's tough," or "He's dangerous," or "He's extremely talented." But ask them to tell you a little bit about the man away from the green-felt tables, and most poker players are stumped.

"I don't really know much about him," one prominent tournament competitor admitted. "He's a mystery."

Another World Champ, who requested anonymity, said, "Huck Seed doesn't say much to anybody. He's sort of anti-social. If you didn't know better, you might think he's got an attitude problem. You would think he's stuck up. I've never had more than two words with him. I guess he's just shy."

Doug Dalton, poker manager at the Mirage, which deals the biggest games in Las Vegas, says Huck Seed is difficult to get close to. "He's very introverted," Dalton says. "After watching him for several years, I've noticed he's one of these people who needs a common ground before he feels comfortable opening up. Huck has one of the characteristics of all the great players: He's focused. The only thing that seems to matter to him is poker. He's very competitive."

According to Jim Albrecht, the long-time poker room manager at Binion's Horseshoe and the tournament director for the World Series of Poker, "Huck Seed is slightly mysterious. He's not like anyone I've known." And Albrecht has known quite a few gamblers in his years at Binion's legendary poker room. Johnny "the Grand Old

Man" Moss, Doyle "Texas Dolly" Brunson, "Amarillo Slim" Preston—all have plied their trade under Albrecht's watchful gaze. "You only see Huck Seed at the table, where he tends to be quiet. I get the feeling he's a loner, that he's not very social. My feeling," Albrecht says, "is that like a lot of brilliant gamblers, his intellect is about a year or two more developed than his emotions. And maybe that's one reason why he's such a phenomenal player."

Few of poker's great players doubt Huck Seed's abilities. Even at age 27, he's shown the world that he can play a difficult complicated game—one that often takes a lifetime to master—as well as anyone on the planet. Phil Hellmuth, who many experts believe may be the most purely gifted poker player in the business, says, "Huck has a tremendous amount of talent. A lot of people, including me, thought he would one day be world champion. The guy is like a freight train, a runaway freight train. He's not afraid to move his chips [make extremely large bets]. And when he's got an open track ahead of him, he tends to run over everything in his path."

But, Hellmuth cautions, runaway trains sometimes crash into walls. "I consider Huck my best friend. And I'm a big fan of his game. He's a very tough, very dangerous player. But he's got to realize, his train hasn't run into any walls yet. I'm one of the people who's wondering what's going to happen when he does."

If Huck Seed crashes and burns, he might do so in a flamboyant manner, losing, say, $1 million in one fateful bad night. He might crumble in a highly public arena, with a crowd of spectators craning to see his every move and television cameras recording his demise for posterity. If, one day, this "runaway train" can no longer take the pressure of high-stakes gambling, he might just self-destruct.

But the smart money isn't betting on that. No, the odds are Huck Seed, whether a World Champion or a flat-broke bum, will quietly accept his fate with grace and dignity, smile bashfully, and disappear into the Vegas night, perched happily on the back of a turnip truck.

* * *

Men "the Master" Nyugen, a world-class champion from Vietnam, who came to America a decade ago on a boat and played his way up to riches and fame, has decided he's fed up with Huck Seed's bullying. As if to say, "Now it's my turn," Men puts in a big raise. Huck Seed, acting last, considers Men's bet, looks at his stack of chips, and "comes over the top," reraising with everything he has, about $500,000.

Without pausing, Men yells, "I've got you! I know you're bluffing. I've got you now! I call!" and shoves all his chips in the pot. Men turns over his cards to reveal A-K of spades, a powerful hold 'em hand.

Huck sheepishly reveals his hand: J-6 off-suit. In fact, he had been bluffing.

"Got you!" the diminutive Men yells, bouncing out of his chair.

The dealer turns the flop: 4,5,7. Huck's six gives him an open-ended straight draw. He needs a three or an eight to win the pot, now well over a million dollars.

The dealer turns a nine. No change. Men is pacing behind his chair, screaming at the cards. "Blank, blank!" He knows that any random card will give him the best hand, an ace-high. Only a jack, six, three, or eight can beat him. Every other card in the deck will knock Seed out of the World Series and render Men Nyugen the dominant force at the final table.

Huck Seed, however, does not move. He does not get out of his chair. He merely stares at the chips on the table.

The dealer turns the final card. It's an eight.

The crowd goes wild. Men lets out an anguished wail. And Huck does nothing but grin, almost imperceptibly. It's not the grin of someone who knows he got miraculously lucky. It's the smile of someone who knows that he's going to win, and nobody can stop him.

25

The (New) Biggest Game in Town

The poker room at the Mirage in Las Vegas is one of those great democratic institutions that pays no heed to race, religion, creed, or social pedigree. Here, it doesn't matter if you're a debt-laden deadbeat, the world's richest man, or something in between: If you have the requisite buy-in—as low as $30—you're welcome to play in this expansive card arena. Poker is color-blind, except for the money-being-green part.

That's why no one who regularly gambles in the Mirage poker room was particularly dumbstruck when Bill Gates wandered in recently to play in the smallest game offered, a $3-$6 limit hold 'em affair. Though the irony of a multi-billionaire gambling with the minimum-wage crowd was lost on no one, the fact that Microsoft's CEO would sate his poker appetite in public, at the Mirage, was no surprise. Hollywood stars (and their gruesome agents), sports heroes (and *their* gruesome agents), titans of industry, Bible Belt politicians—all of them come through here on an almost daily basis.

Sure, it's always exciting to see one of the most powerful men in the world get his two pair snapped off by a grandmother from Ohio. But to poker cognoscenti, the real drama was unfolding in the corner of the room, behind the velvet ropes, next to the sign that says, "Please do not stand in this area," where seven locals and a wealthy visitor were conducting the Big Game.

Typically, the Big Game, where the wins and losses regularly run into six and seven figures, resembles a school of sharks dismembering an unfortunate baitfish. Today, though, the baitfish of the moment, a flamboyant Aussie, had grown fangs, and the sharks were looking for a place to hide.

Several years ago the estimable author Al Alvarez wrote a revealing account of high-stakes poker in Las Vegas called *The Biggest Game in Town*. In his book, originally a series of articles in *The New Yorker*, Alvarez introduced readers to some of poker's heaviest hitters, a coterie of seasoned road gamblers and brilliant card sharps, reckless plungers and savant-like prodigies, who thought nothing of playing for pots the size (and value) of a 1979 Cadillac.

Some of the colorful gamblers from *The Biggest Game in Town*, like legendary two-time World Champion Doyle Brunson, still play in the Big Game. Others have died. Most, however, have been supplanted by a new breed of player: The regular combatants in today's biggest game in town are generally younger, better educated, and more private than their forebears. They're less inclined to publicize their poker triumphs and less likely to fire the public's imagination. They don't publish how-to books or make appearances on late-night talk shows. They simply play poker—quite well, and for quite incomprehensible stakes.

Recently, before his untimely death last year, an enormously wealthy businessman from Paris, known throughout Las Vegas as "the Frenchman," inspired the biggest poker game in America. He liked to play hold 'em. He liked to play hold 'em for astonishingly large stakes, like $2,000-$4,000 a bet. The local experts happily obliged, and the Frenchman often dropped $1 million or more per visit. Before him there was the Southern Gentleman, the scion of a prominent Confederate family. The Gentleman preferred good old-fashioned seven-card stud, the game his grandpappy played. The local experts happily obliged, and the Southern Gentleman often dropped $1 million or more per visit. Before him there was the Movie Producer, and before him the Publisher, and before him a long legacy of brave visitors who wanted to play real big. The locals always obliged.

These days, most of the players in the Big Game just want to be left alone, free to ply their lucrative trade. (At their request, names and identifying details have been changed for this story.) But like the old-timers, the new breed plays in public, here at the corner table of the Mirage poker room. Anyone who wants to see the largest casino ring game in America can stop over and take a good look at the action, though if you tarry too long an officious employee with a clipboard and a regretful smile will politely tell you, "I'm sorry, we can't have anyone standing here."

Like fish need water, the Big Game needs a fish. There wouldn't *be* a game if not for the presence of an "honored guest." The locals figure there's no point in playing against each other: They'd just be passing the money back and forth, gambling without a discernible edge. They need a soft spot in the game, just one. Because when you play high enough, one producer is sufficient to feed the whole game. Divide $3 million six ways and you've got a nice week's salary.

The generous visitor is the game's fuel. Be he the former governor of a southern state or a billionaire industrialist with an utter disregard for money, his presence compels the best (and best-financed) poker players in Las Vegas to make the corner table at the Mirage their office until the visitor is ready to return home—usually after a week or so, with a million or two dollars less than when he arrived. Whether a well-known celebrity or an otherwise anonymous member of a laudatory *Forbes* list, the game's honored guest usually *feels* honored. He's honored just to be playing with the gang of heavy hitters that nearly everyone in poker considers the biggest talents in the game. Unlike tennis or basketball or hockey, where even being super-rich does not allow you to compete against the game's best practitioners, poker affords anyone with the courage and the bankroll the privilege of playing with the superstars.

It's an ego thing.

Some of the out-of-towners who take a shot at the Big Game believe they may have the skills and stamina and character to win. Some aren't sure, but intend to find out. And others know they're not very good. They just want to be able to say they played with the great ones—and had a good time.

This week at the Mirage, the visitor—call him "the Aussie"—is a magnificently rich restaurant magnate from Melbourne who considers poker his second favorite hobby, after big-game hunting. "These days it's easier to find a good poker game than to shoot an elephant," he cackles, tucking a long lock of auburn hair behind his ear.

To his delight the Aussie finds himself competing against the usual Las Vegas suspects: "the Wonk," a lean, impeccably groomed software-designer-turned-gambler; "Big Ricky," who gave up a lucrative rare-coin business for an even more lucrative career in poker; the "Philanderer," who finances his expensive taste in wives at the gaming tables; the "Pretty Boy," a former model who has parlayed his family's trust fund into a seat with the big boys; the "Hick," who has built the profits from his chain of Midwestern sporting goods stores into a formidable poker bankroll; the "Gamesman," an internationally recognized bridge and backgammon expert whose love of games led him to the most dangerous one of all; and the "Bruiser," a waif-like, wisp of a man who is often called the best all-around player in poker. Four other professionals, including a couple of middle-limit players hoping to take a once-a-year shot at the big time, have their name on the waiting list.

You can almost taste the anticipation, the barely restrained urge to begin the hunt. One pro tells me that this particular game, even for the corner table of the Mirage, is unusual. "Normally the biggest game in here is maybe one-tenth the size of this game. This is a two- or three-times-a-year kind of occurrence. Except for when Archie, the seventeen-million-dollar man, was playing everyone heads-up,

I haven't seen a game like this in a while, not since the Frenchman."

The form of poker they play is whatever the Aussie feels like playing. During his last visit several months ago, it was $2,000-$4,000 seven-card stud. Today it is pot-limit Omaha. The ante is $500. The blinds—compulsory bets made without looking at one's hand—are $1,000-$2,000. The maximum bet is the size of the pot or $75,000, whichever is less. The buy-in is $100,000, though most players start with at least double that.

Whereas most poker games are accompanied by the staccato clatter of ceramic chips hitting the pot, the Big Game's sound is augmented by the dull thud of bundled $100 bills being blithely tossed onto the green felt.

According to one pro on the waiting list, it's impossible for the honored guest to select a game where he has the advantage: The superstars of Las Vegas are good at *all* forms of poker. But the Aussie's choice, pot-limit Omaha, may be the worst possible alternative. "This game will give the amateur player a repeatedly bad price [odds] on his hand, and he won't ever know it," the pro whispers. "Some other games the Aussie might have a chance to get lucky. But this one? Almost no chance."

If the Aussie has any edge, the pro says, it's his physical conditioning. "If he's stuck, he can play thirty-six hours straight. Time-wise, this guy can play us into the ground. Just like he respects our skills, we respect his fortitude. There's not many people who can stay awake that long, let alone play decent poker. Besides that, though, I don't see how he could beat this game."

How about by getting lucky? To the chagrin of the assembled experts, the Aussie begins his planned three-week stay in Las Vegas with four consecutive winning sessions. Though he plays nearly every hand dealt to him—a sure recipe for financial disaster—the Aussie is pounding the game, scooping up $20,000 pots as if they were so many stray quarters. In a typical encounter, a pro raises the pot; the Aussie calls. After the community cards are distributed the pro bets again; the Aussie raises him back the size of the pot, or in some cases, $75,000. Most of the time the pro, not wanting to risk the price of a new Mercedes, surrenders. When the pro decides to play on with the Aussie, more often than not the gleeful visitor shows his hosts the better hand.

After two eight-hour sessions, the Aussie is up more than $900,000. Big Ricky is not amused.

"I had a made flush on the flop," Ricky complains, recalling one particularly painful hand. "The guy calls me with a pair. Just a pair! There's a flush out there staring him in the face and he calls all his money with a pair. Next card gives him two pair. Next card gives him a full house. Two perfect running cards to beat me. You see what we're dealing with here?"

With each small victory the Aussie neither gloats nor apologizes. He just keeps playing, hand after hand, rubbing a polished set of rosary beads in his left palm. When he becomes tired, or perhaps when he feels his fortunes may be turning, he stacks up his bundles of bills and $5,000 chips in a plastic rack and bids his famous hosts good night. They tell him they look forward to playing with him tomorrow, in the morning. "Yes, me too," the Aussie says, and disappears with their money.

In the Hollywood version of this story the Aussie would continue to win, breaking the Wonk and the Gamesman and the Pretty Boy and all the rest of the sharks, until only he and the putative champ, the Bruiser, were left. They would then play heads-up, famous pro versus wily amateur, until the Bruiser, down nearly $4 million, concedes the game to our unknown hero, telling the Aussie he is surely the finest poker player to have ever visited Las Vegas. At which point the Aussie would reveal he is not actually an Aussie at all, but a mid-limit grinder from the Mirage's $50-100 game, an astute observer who's studied the Big Game from nearby for three years, memorizing each player's weakness, planning a grand assault. Or some such nonsense.

Alas, this is not Movieland. It is Las Vegas, where the cruel mathematics of the edge eventually crush even the luckiest gambler, no matter how many restaurants he owns back in Melbourne.

At his zenith, the Aussie is $1.2 million to the good. By the time he gets back on his jet to the land of kangaroos, he's donated several million dollars to the local economy.

And, honestly, he doesn't really mind. He's had fun. He's had the best poker players in the world perplexed, anxious, *down*. He's been treated like a royal ambassador. He's felt the elation of triumph and the sting of failure. And more than anything else, he's been one of the boys, a temporary member in one of the most elite clubs in Las Vegas. He's played in the biggest game in town.

26

The Hand You're Dealt

I didn't win the main event at the World Series of Poker this year. I'm not the reigning world champion. I'm not $1 million richer. (All of which should be obvious, since I am writing this story instead of luxuriating on some Caribbean island with my new best friend the showgirl.) But along with thousands of other poker players—hardened professionals and serious amateurs alike—I *tried* to do all these things. And you can, too.

Which is why the World Series of Poker may be the most democratic sporting event on the planet. Anyone with a little money, a lot of gambling talent, and a highly developed capacity for dreaming can do what I do every year: go to Binion's Horseshoe, enter a modestly priced ($220) satellite tournament, and, by winning said tournament, earn a seat in the big dance, the $10,000-buy-in World Championship. First place in the main event, a four-day odyssey that in 1997 attracted 312 entrants, is $1 million. Second paid $583,000. And for players who finished as low as 27th, the prize was $21,200.

Every type of poker game is played at the World Series of Poker, including various forms of stud and draw. But the king of games, the one used to decide the World Championship itself, is called "no-limit Texas hold 'em." The "no-limit" means you can bet any or all of your chips at any time, a delightful rule that, in recent years, has created a number of million-dollar pots, hands of poker on which a million dollars is riding. Texas hold 'em is played every day of the year at Los Angeles card casinos like Hollywood Park, the Commerce, and the Bicycle Club, and these are the places where I honed my game, preparing myself for the fiercest poker competition on the planet: guys with lots of gold jewelry, inscrutable faces, and nicknames like "the Master."

Sharpies.

After many years as a gambling columnist, I figured it was time for me to take my place among the wiseguys.

I arrive at the Horseshoe three days before the start of the World Championship event, allowing myself three shots (and a couple thousand dollars) at winning a satellite tournament, three shots at earning a ticket to the most important congregation in poker.

It does not immediately strike me as ominous foreshadowing when on my first hand—the very first hand I'm dealt at the World Series of Poker—I lose all my chips, all $200 of them. Having raised before "the flop" (the displaying of the community upcards) with a pair of jacks, I end up donating my entire stack of money to a foolish chain-smoking Vietnamese lad who has called me with a pair of fives. When a five comes on the last card, the river, as poker players say, giving him 3-of-a-kind, I'm left with nothing but a blank strip of green felt where once my chips sat so hopefully.

"Unlucky," I think, reminding myself that if it were not for the occasional bolt of fortune, lesser players would never compete in poker tournaments. Why should they? The better players would always win. Indeed, luck is inherent to poker. But unlike, say, in baccarat or craps, skill is the game's primary ingredient, especially at the World Series of Poker, where several expert players like Johnny Moss, Doyle Brunson, and Johnny Chan have won multiple World Championships. As I hand the dealer $200 more (players may rebuy at a satellite tournament during the first hour of play), I tell myself to remain equanimous, to handle the bad luck with grace. Good fortune will eventually come my way.

I continue to tell myself this, mantra-like, as I watch three more stacks of $200 disappear down the gullets of three other voracious players. Each time I begin with the strongest hand—every two-card combination is either a favorite or an underdog, depending on what it's up against—and each time an opponent with a weaker hand spanks me hard.

I hold ace-king; a gargantuan Floridian, scratching his head and chewing on a toothpick, holds ace-queen. The flop comes king-jack-10, and he makes a straight.

I hold a pair of nines; a relic from the age of disco, sporting smoked sunglasses, a silk shirt, and a diamond pinkie ring, calls my raise with an ace-9: An ace comes on the flop, and he's happy as a Bee-Gee.

And most preposterously, both I and my opponent, an unreadable English fellow who plays poker while listening to Mozart through tiny headphones, hold identical hands, a pair of tens. I've got the black ones; he's got the red ones. Surely we'll split the pot. Alas, four diamonds come on the board. He makes a flush.

I try to be philosophical: These things happen. But then self-pity inevitably rears its ugly head: "But why do they have to happen to me? Especially when I'm trying to win the World Series of Poker! It's not fair!"

Down $800 and feeling inordinately sorry for myself, I go to the Horseshoe's famous coffee shop and drown my sorrows in red meat and pumpkin pie.

* * *

My second attempt at winning the world title starts promisingly. Stung by the previous evening's debacle, I play very "tight," folding speculative drawing hands and betting aggressively when I'm holding something powerful. For the first hour, while the wild gamblers around me are calling and raising with just about anything, hoping to go "on a rush," I sit patiently, monk-like, and wait, paying my antes and observing the mayhem. Just when I think I can

231

no longer stand the monotony, I'm dealt a juicy hand, the ace-king of spades. I bet it strongly and get called in two spots. When the flop brings a rash of baby cards, my ace-king holds up and I've tripled my stack.

This happens about four more times. Each hand I start with an odds-on favorite and finish with the money, the way it's supposed to work in a kind and just world.

Three hours into the satellite tournament, the field has been narrowed from 120 to 36. The final 11 survivors will earn seats in the World Championship. I've built my original $220 buy-in up to $4,700. The promised land is within sight.

And then I look down to find what I've been waiting for all night: a monster. I've been dealt two kings, the second most powerful starting hand in Texas hold 'em. I hope to get into a raising war with preferably one other opponent, someone who thinks he's holding real power, only to discover that the wily journalist from Los Angeles, the one who's been playing so patiently, so precisely, is holding the hammer. My wish comes true. I raise. A pro down at the other end of the table, one of the top players in Maryland, considers his hand for a moment and raises me back. I re-raise him, pushing my entire stack of chips toward the center of the table.

"All in," the dealer announces.

Without hesitation, the Maryland pro pushes all his chips toward the middle. There's close to $10,000 in the pot.

I can think of only five hands the pro could have called with. "I got aces," he says, flipping up his cards. And that's the one hand I didn't want to see. My kings are the second most powerful starting combination; his aces are the first.

Now only two cards in the deck can help me. I need to get lucky.

The miracle I need to stay in the tournament does not materialize. As the dealer pushes the mountain of chips toward the pro, the pile of hundreds that will surely earn him a seat in the World Championship, the pro shrugs at me and says, "Bad luck."

I nod silently and make a hurried exit, trying mightily to honor an age-old credo: Real men do not cry at the poker table.

Yes, bad luck, indeed, I think, calculating the probability of another player holding aces when I'm holding kings. It's a complicated proposition, but depending on how you figure it, the odds are as low as 25-1 or as high as 5,600-1. (A regular tournament player later tells me it's happened to him four times—and he's been playing for 20 years.) I trudge off to my room, feeling like there's a sticky film of misfortune clinging to my back.

But on my final satellite attempt, the night before the main event begins, everything goes wonderfully, joyously, *right*. I'm reading my opponents like their cards were turned face up. I'm getting rid of weak hands precisely the moment *before* they get me in trouble. I'm milking my strong hands for every dollar they're worth.

I'm playing like someone who belongs in the main event at the World Series of Poker.

Indeed, I single-handedly dispatch six players from the tournament, stacking their chips on my expanding pile, growing like a happy hog. As each busted player exits, another comes to fill the empty seat. Soon thereafter I bust him, too.

"Guy's a terminator," someone sighs.

Just then, a new player is parked at my table. Literally.

A young man with a ponytail and alligator boots wheels a hospital gurney to my table. On it is a man of indeterminate age in worse shape than I've ever seen any living person.

Whether because of a debilitating degenerative disease or a profound birth defect, this poker player has essentially been reduced to a head on a stretcher. His torso, or what's left of it, is about the size of a large cat. He does not appear to have legs. The one arm I can make out is as thin as a pool cue and as short as your forearm. His mouth is frozen open in a perpetual gasp.

I know I am supposed to be evolved and educated and

politically correct enough that I should not feel revulsion and pity and horror at the sight of this man, this head on a stretcher. I know I am supposed to be able to look beyond his disfigurement and see the humanity within. I know I am supposed to treat him as I would any other poker player. But I can't. I can't even look at him.

Suddenly, I want to be anywhere but here at Binion's Horseshoe, playing in the World Series of Poker. I want to dance and run and make love. I want to do all the mundane and wondrous things the man on the gurney will never do. Trapped on a stretcher, imprisoned in a body that will not cooperate, this man cannot dance and run and make love. He can only lie on his bed and watch.

And play poker. His ponytailed assistant holds his cards for him and, when instructed, bets for him. The disfigured man takes in everything, assessing his opponents with a firm, observant gaze that they dare not fix on him.

I need to last only an hour or two more and I'll be in the million-dollar main event. But I know that will not happen.

I know I will eventually confront the man on the gurney across from me, and I know he will bust me. I know I will not win the World Championship. I know I will leave the Binion's Horseshoe poker room shaken and slightly nauseous. Yet I also know I will not curse the whims of fate, the unseen forces that gave the winning cards to someone else.

I know I will lose this game of poker. And I will feel like the luckiest man in the world.

About Huntington Press

Huntington Press is a specialty publisher of Las Vegas- and gambling-related books and periodicals. To receive a copy of the Huntington Press catalog, call 1-800-244-2224 or write to the address below.

Huntington Press
3687 South Procyon Avenue
Las Vegas, Nevada 89103